Kyrock

A

Pictorial

History

Ernie Elmore

i

Kyrock A Pictorial History

ISBN-13: 978-1534881259

ISBN-10: 1534881255

TABLE OF CONTENTS

Chapter 1   **Introduction**

Kyrock Plant Circa 1925

This photograph was taken about 1925 when the Kentucky Rock Asphalt Company was going "full steam" providing jobs and resulting in a flourishing economy in Edmonson County Kentucky.

Steam from the power plant (seen rising in the center of photo) was piped to the primary crusher on the lower right where large boulders of asphalt rock were pulverized and sent by a conveyor belt to the crushing plant where it was further pulverized. It was then transferred and loaded onto barges located on a canal. A dredge boat maneuvered the barges to the Nolin River (center right) where they were picked up for tow by a fleet of steam boats for transport to the distribution center in Bowling Green, Kentucky. In the center of the photo can be seen the Kyrock Commissary and the ice plant. To the left of the steam plant are the swinging bridge, barn and area residences for plant personnel. At the top of Blue Hill (upper left) is the hotel.

The plant was moved about five miles to this location near Nolin River from the Wadsworth Stone and Paving Company location on Green River about 1919.

Chapter 1   **Introduction**

When preparing this account of Kyrock I wondered at times if it might be only another version of previous publications, of which there are many excellent ones. As I poured through the reference materials it became apparent to me that they were all that remained of a time that made an indelible mark on the part of Kentucky where my roots ran so deep. Many people in Edmonson County Kentucky were affected in some manner by the presence of the Kyrock plant. Both of my grandfathers, my uncle, many relatives as well as my wife's father and many of her relatives were at one time employed at the plant. As memories fade and those who lived and worked at Kyrock pass away all that is left to help us remember this important part of our local history are these kinds of publications. Pictures fade or are lost and many artifacts are misplaced. The buildings and landmarks eventually disappear leaving only distant memories by those who are left that were fortunate to have seen and experience the times when Kyrock was a bustling community. Eventually there will only be these publications to let others see and understand what happened there. I realized that any efforts that would help preserve the memories and history of Kyrock would be worth the time I spent on it even if some of the material in my account might at times duplicate that from other publications.

My intent for this publication is to provide an accurate and thorough description of the people, work and activities as well as a description of how the area would have looked during the time Kentucky Rock Asphalt Company was in operation.

Most of the materials available for reference were newspaper or magazine articles, college publications, Kyrock publications and private accounts or interviews with those familiar with Kyrock. My goal was to take all these references and make one publication containing as much information as possible from them. The photographs included in this publication were taken from several sources. Most

Chapter 1   **Introduction**

were provided from private collections while others came from history archives and previous publications. While attempts were made to provide the clearest copy possible, some photos were very old and in poor condition. I have tried to include as many photos as possible even when there was very little information available on some of them.

Hopefully this publication will serve as an accurate historical account that does not replace but rather adds to previous publications by others. As you read and browse through the pictures let yourself be taken back to a time when people around Kyrock worked hard and treated their fellow workers and neighbors with respect. Try to sense the love and togetherness that people felt for those in the community. My hope is that you might come away with a better understanding of those who lived and worked at Kyrock.

Chapter 2 Discovery and Development

Indians discovered a black tarry substance in the rocks and cliffs of western Kentucky long before the settlers began their excursions into this region. The substance was found to naturally ooze from these rocks making it readily available to be scrapped away and used for sealing the cracks and holes in the Indians canoes used to carry them up and down Nolin and Green River. They also used the material for medicinal purposes to seal wounds no doubt suffered from their enemies. When settlers did begin to move into the region they found the substance to be useful in waterproofing boats and sealing cracks in their cabins learning this application from the Indians. The Kentucky Geological Survey of 1854 mentions a "black rock" and "coal tar" found in the western Kentucky region in Edmonson County which was the asphalt rock typically found in the area. The "black rock" was distinguishable from coal because it was found to be high grade silica that was covered with the black tarry material. Engineers began to hear of these reports and realize that the material might have some marketable properties if it could be excavated from the rugged terrain and moved to other areas. Rock asphalt had been used in Europe in the early 19th century to cover roads but it was in the 1870's to 1880's that the first roads were paved in the United States using the European material and at a considerable expense. In the 1880's engineers in this country attempted the commercial development of the large deposits of rock asphalt. In 1889 tests were conducted when a stretch of road was laid on 18th Avenue North in Nashville, Tennessee using rock asphalt taken from Edmonson County Kentucky. The success of this project showed much promise for the product leading to other paving projects. In the 1890's representatives of the Wadsworth Stone and Paving Company of Pittsburg, Pennsylvania began marketing the material for road surfaces and in 1904 opened a quarry on the Green River near Brownsville.

Chapter 2   Discovery and Development

Brief History of Kyrock

LONG years ago before the first party of white settlers found their way through the opening in the blue wall at Cumberland Gap, Cherokee squaws, roaming through the hills which now echo to the hum of the white man's industry, around the busy little town of Kyrock, in Edmonson County, Kentucky, scraped away the asphalt ooze that bled from outcropping rich spots in the underlying asphalt rock, and used the pitch to calk the seams of the bark canoes which carried the Cherokee braves down the Nolin and Green Rivers into the camps of their hostile neighbors. And Cherokee medicine men scraped away the pungent pitch to patch the arrow rents in the skins of such of the braves as returned.

White settlers, following in the wake of Boone and the earlier pioneers, learned of its location and its utility from the retreating red men.

Later came men with knowledge to read the earth's signs, and, being wise to man's growing needs, they pronounced it good for purposes other than chalking canoes and salving wounds. Then, considering the remoteness of that tangle of wooded hills and rocky ravines, they sighed and left it. And due to the inaccessibility of the region, no other than these simple uses were made of this rich store of nature's bounty until within comparatively recent years, when the work of the federal government, in cleaning up Green River and its tributaries, made possible the commercial development of these rich deposits of what engineers pronounce the finest paving material yet discovered.

It took unusual engineering skill and financial daring to open up the Kyrock deposits so that this natural paving material could be delivered on the roads and streets in such quantities and at a price that would be commercially practicable.

The excerpt above was taken from a book by Kentucky Rock Asphalt Company called "The Kyrock Book" believed to have been published sometime in the mid 1920's. It describes how asphalt in western Kentucky was discovered.

Chapter 2 **Discovery and Development**

Canoe Sealed With Tar

This drawing of a canoe shows how it might have looked after it was sealed with the tar from asphalt rock. The "Kyrock Book" produced by Kentucky Rock Asphalt around 1928 described how the Indians discovered a practical use for the tar found around Kyrock.

Native American Indians "scraped away the asphalt ooze that bled from outcropping rich spots in the underlying asphalt rock, and used the pitch to calk the seams of the bark canoes which carried the Cherokee braves down the Nolin and Green Rivers into the camps of their "hostile neighbors." It lasted longer than the tree gum typically used on canoes that had to be cleaned and softened before use.

White men learned from the Indians of the tar's water sealing properties and also used it for salving on wounds.

Chapter 2 Discovery and Development

Early Photo of Brownsville, Kentucky

This photograph of Brownsville was taken in 1907 by Borst Photo from what was known as Reservoir Hill. It was distributed by Ruble B. Cowles when he was Property Valuation Administrator. In the center of the photo is the Dunn Hotel on the left side of Cross Main Street and the Reed Hotel is on the right side. The brick building in the center was the A.A. Demunbrun Store and later the Woodcock's Western Auto Store. The large house on the hill was built by Mr. and Mrs. J.P. Reed. The building to the right of (and behind) the Reed Hotel was the Star Livery Stable which was operated by Mr. Reed and his sons.

The main business block included the Ed Lindsey Store and the Brownsville Deposit Bank (three story building) on the right side of the street. On the left side of the street was the Edmonson County Courthouse.

The white two story frame building at the extreme lower right facing Washing Street housed lawyers' offices and a barber shop run by Edgar Page. Private schools were also conducted in this building.

Chapter 2 **Discovery and Development**

As automobiles began to become more popular in the early 1900's the demand for asphalt for paving roads began to take hold. Sometime during the time period between 1900 and 1918 the federal government worked on a major project to clean up the Green River and its tributaries which made it much easier and economical to make shipments up Nolin and Green Rivers. These two things spurred development of the quarry and activities rapidly began to take place to acquire mineral rights with stock shares, buy land and begin mining the asphalt. In 1906 Judge Marvel Mills Logan, who at the time was county judge and later became a U.S. Senator, helped to acquire 45,000 acres of land and in 1917 he organized the Bee Spring Land and Mining Company. In the same year this company merged with Wadsworth Stone and Paving Company to form the Kentucky Rock Asphalt Company. A quarry was opened on the Nolin River and a rock crushing plant was built there in 1918. So began the establishment of Kyrock, located about 35 miles from Bowling Green, Kentucky and about six miles from Brownsville, Kentucky near the Green River. The impact of this new company would result in the creation of Kyrock community in Edmonson County and had a dramatic impact on the region. The "black rock" discovered in the mid 1800's was found by geologists to consist of sandstone impregnated with bitumen (tar) and was ideal for paving roads. The bituminous rock was located in an area known as the "Pottsville conglomerate sandstone of the Pennsylvanian system". More recently the bituminous rock has been referred to as "tar sands" and stated to be located along the southeastern rim of the Eastern Interior Basin. This area includes Edmonson County Kentucky where large deposits of this material with ideal bitumen content are located. The bitumen content of the tar sands mined in Edmonson County typically ranged from

Chapter 2 Discovery and Development

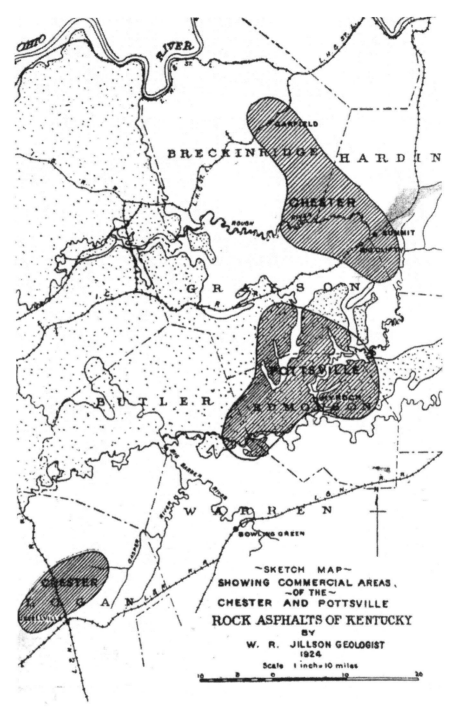

This map shows where the rock asphalt deposits were located in Edmonson County Kentucky.

Map was taken from the Mary E. Marks dissertation at University of Chicago 1931.

Chapter 2   Discovery and Development

6 to 10%. The preferred bitumen content for Kyrock asphalt was found to be about 7% when used for paving roads.

An interesting story was told by Judge Marvel Mills Logan in which he described how it was discovered that the rock asphalt could be "laid cold".   When the Wadsworth Stone and Paving Company opened a quarry near Brownsville, Kentucky in the 1890's he relayed the following story:

"Rock asphalt as now used for road surfacing is spread in the condition in which it comes from the mill. The asphalt is spread cold over the base to be covered and it is then rolled with a very heavy roller which reduces its thickness about half. Under the pressure of the roller it is bonded into a condition approaching it original state. The discovery of the possibility of its use in this way was made by accident. It was hauled in wheelbarrows from the mill to the boat. Some rock asphalt spilled on the path over which it was being carried, the wheelbarrow passing over it, pressed it back into solid form. This fact was noted and experimentation showed that the rock asphalt laid cold could be rolled into an excellent road surfacing as a result."

The real growth of the asphalt industry at Kyrock was spurred by the increasing popularity of automobiles increasing demand for rock asphalt for paving roads in primarily urban areas. Eventually the need for better roads became a nationwide phenomenon and many states developed programs for new road construction. In 1901 the production of rock asphalt nationwide was only 4,000 tons, but by 1928 this had risen to 400,000 tons. This increase was spurred by a five million dollar investment in Edmonson County Kentucky and the opening of Kyrock in 1918. From 1918 to 1928 the amount of rock asphalt shipped down Green River

Chapter 2 **Discovery and Development**

As judge in Edmonson County Marvel Mills Logan was inspirational in helping obtain land for Kyrock Asphalt Company.

Marvel Mills Logan *Marvel Mills Logan (January 7, 1874 – October 3, 1939), a Democrat, served as a member of the United States Senate from Kentucky.*

Mills was born on a farm near Brownsville, Edmonson County, Kentucky. He taught school for two years and also conducted a training school for teachers. He then studied law and was admitted to the bar in 1896. He practiced law in Brownsville. He served as chairman of the board of trustees of Brownsville; as county attorney of Edmonson County 1902-1903; as assistant Attorney General of Kentucky 1912-1915; as Attorney General of Kentucky 1915-1917; and as chairman of the Kentucky Tax Commission 1917-1918. Mills then moved to Louisville, Kentucky in 1918 and then to Bowling Green, Kentucky in 1922, continuing to practice law. He served as a member of the State Board of Education, the State Board of Sinking Fund Commissioners, and the State Board of Printing Commissioners. He served as a justice of the Kentucky Court of Appeals 1926-1930 and as Chief Justice in 1931.

Mills was elected as a Democrat to the United States Senate in 1930 and reelected in 1936 and served from March 4, 1931, until his death. While in the Senate he served as Chairman of the Committee on Mines and Mining (Seventy-third through Seventy-fifth Congresses) and on the Committee on Claims (Seventy-sixth Congress).

In 1933 Logan chaired the subcommittee dispatched to Louisiana by the United States Senate to investigate allegations of corrupt activities of the political machine of Huey Long during the 1932 election of John H. Overton to the Senate. Logan's inquiry reported that the election was impacted by fraud, specifically the involvement of dummy candidates and deducts (money taken from public employees' pay for use by the Long machine), but no action was taken against Overton.

Logan died in Washington, D.C. on October 3, 1939 and is buried in the Logan family cemetery near Brownsville.

Chapter 2 Discovery and Development

increased by more than 300,000 tons, most of this increase attributed to production at Kyrock.

There were many obstacles to establishing the rock asphalt industry in Edmonson County. The area where quarries were built was in a rugged, isolated area with little access by road and none by rail. There were high narrow ridges and deep v-shaped valleys or hollows. Veins of asphalt were usually located near the tops of these high narrow ridges. Roads into the area were dirt and became nearly impass-able after heavy rains or during winter months. In the 1920's the road leading northwest from the Dixie Highway (US 31W) to the county seat of Brownsville was a dirt or gravel road surface. After passing through Brownsville the road led to the Green River where a ferry could be taken toward Kyrock. The road contin-ued north-northwest to the Kyrock Road where the area became somewhat rugged. Once you reached the site of the quarry the road was paved with asphalt and it was obvious that a large scale operation was present. Houses were concentrated in small communities within the Kyrock area outside the quarry and plant operations. Since using the roads to transport tons of rock asphalt was out of the question and no railroad was available, other means of transportation had to be obtained. When the Nolin and Green Rivers were cleared by the federal government, Kyrock gained access to a suitable shipping method for their product. Kyrock took ad-vantage of these newly navigable waterways by establishing a transport system using barges pulled by stern-wheel steamboats. The barges were loaded on or near the Nolin River next to the processing plant and transported up the Nolin River to Green River and eventually up the Barren River to its distribution points in either Bowling Green or Rockport. Utilizing this method of shipment of the rock asphalt

Chapter 2 Discovery and Development

The top photo shows what Hwy. 259 looked like after leaving Brownsville before reaching Green River. The Green River Ferry had to transport cars across the river to continue on towards Kyrock. The bottom photo shows Hwy. 259 (once called B&R Road for Brownsville-Rocky Hill Road), a dirt road around 1914, leading from the Brownsville Ferry on to Kyrock. A horseback rider is approaching a barn in the center of the photo.

Chapter 2   Discovery and Development

was a practical solution to transportation difficulties from the rugged terrain around Kyrock.

Another obstacle that had to be overcome was how rock asphalt could be mined from the quarries and then processed to a consistency fine enough to be used for road building. In the beginning of the development of the rock asphalt industry mining and processing was done primarily by manual labor. Large boulders had to be excavated and broken up manually prior to further milling and crushing. Eventually steam driven mining and processing equipment became available to assist in getting to the rock asphalt and removing the large boulders to a crusher. All this equipment was required to be brought down the river by barge to the Kyrock plant. The prime rock asphalt layer which was usually about 20 feet thick was covered with a layer of dirt, shale and sandstone that could be 40 to 60 feet deep. This layer of "overburden" had to be removed by first blasting it with dynamite and then breaking it up into pieces small enough to haul away. The layer of rock asphalt also had to be blasted with dynamite to break it up into pieces that could be loaded into containers. Moving the rock from quarry to crushers was initially done by using road wagons or skip boxes pulled over tracks. Eventually, locomotives called "dinkeys" were used to pull small open box cars of the rock to the crushers. Once the rock was loaded into the crusher a series of other crushers, mills and grinders were used as the product traveled on a conveyor where it was pulverized until the correct consistency was achieved. This pulverized rock asphalt then had to be blended to give a product with a consistent bitumen content of about 7%. Sampling and testing of the rock asphalt had to be performed at frequent stages in the process to assure that all the specifications were being met.

Chapter 2   Discovery and Development

There were no public utilities such as electricity and water available in the Kyrock area. Electricity had to be generated by the company for plant operations and buildings. Coal was brought in by barge to fire steam engines that were used for electricity and plant equipment. Water used for the plant was pumped from the Nolin River. A suitable workforce had to be recruited and trained to perform many types of work that they were unaccustomed to doing. Housing and supplies were necessary for the hundreds of workers and their families. Accomplishing these things was no easy matter requiring the skills and personality of just the right person to lead the effort.

Brief History of Kyrock

Careful exploration of the territory and analysis of the various deposits to determine their suitability for paving purposes led to the selection of the present Kyrock holdings which are located in Edmonson County, slightly west of the geographical center of Kentucky, near the famous Mammoth Cave and in the geological formation known as the Pottsville sands.

This section of Kentucky, owing to its unsuitability for farming, is but sparsely settled. The region is hilly—almost mountainous, and until recent years was covered with heavy forest and dense undergrowth.

Shovels, locomotives, cars, and other equipment needed to clear the land and remove the heavy overburden were, of necessity, barged over the long and tortuous water route from Bowling Green. Then came the problem of labor—men to do the work and a place for them to live.

To produce Kyrock it was necessary to build a town—in the wilderness. Today it is a thriving little village of about two thousand inhabitants, all housed in comfortable homes, the more important buildings being lighted by electricity and heated by steam. The children are educated in a modern, progressive school. A community church furnishes the center for religious interest and activity. A modernly stocked general store supplies everything in the line of necessities, and a surprising array of luxuries. In addition to which there is a moving picture theatre, community buildings, recreation grounds and other interests that contribute to the social activity, comfort, happiness, and contentment of the inhabitants. Several years ago the Government established a post office in the center of this interesting community and called the town "Kyrock."

The excerpt above was taken from a book by Kentucky Rock Asphalt Company called "The Kyrock Book" believed to have been published sometime in the mid 1920's. It describes how asphalt in western Kentucky was discovered.

Chapter 3   Mr. Carmichael

In 1919 after formation of Kyrock it was temporarily run by General Superintendent and Manager Mr. L.P. Johnson. The newly formed company needed a person who had experience and knowledge of not only mining techniques but also had the disposition to direct a workforce composed of people unaccustomed to working in a demanding mining and processing company. They found a perfect fit in such a person when they hired Mr. Henry St. George Tucker Carmichael.

Henry St. George Tucker Carmichael was hired in 1919 to run the newly formed Kyrock Asphalt Company. He had a degree in civil engineering from Washington Lee University. His knowledge and experience as well as his personality were a perfect fit for Kyrock.

He came from a well-respected family that had migrated from Augusta, Georgia to Lexington, Virginia in the 1800's. Harry Carmichael was what he preferred to be called but was respectfully called "Mr. Carmichael" by everyone around Kyrock. He graduated from Washington Lee University in 1899 with a degree in civil engineering and a thorough knowledge of geology. In 1900 he began working for B&O Railroad in their engineering department and gained extensive experience the next few years on large projects connected to some of the country's largest railroad systems. From 1910 to 1912 he worked as superintendent of construction and assistant manager on portions of the eighty mile stretch of railroad near Pittsburg helping connect a transcontinental rail system. In 1912 he joined the Mason & Hanger Company of Richmond, Kentucky working in surveying and building railroads in the coal fields of West Virginia and Pennsylvania. During this time Mason Hanger was selected by the U.S. government as the largest contractor to help build the Old Hickory Powder Plant just outside Nashville, Tennessee. The newly hired Harry Carmichael was sent there to work on construction of the new plant but after it was completed he was requested by the Secretary of War to ramain at that facility as an explosives foreman. At that time there were no plants producing gun powder in quantities needed for World War I. The new plant was an enormous undertaking that involved construction of buildings and houses for workers, commissaries, restaurants, post office, new roads, railroads, water, electricity and things too numerous to mention. In all, Mason Hanger built more than 2500 buildings at the facility. Harry Carmichael had gained an enormous amount of knowledge and experience working at the new plant. When the war armistice was announced in November of 1918 production of gun powder at the facility was halted two months later and this likely prompted him to accept an offer to become the new superintendent of Kyrock. This decision to accept the job at Kyrock was a life changing one not only in the life of Mr. Carmichael but also in the lives of many others living in the area around Kyrock. In 1923 the powder plant was sold to Dupont Chemical Company who converted it to a rayon production plant. In 1924 nearly half of the plant was destroyed by fire. But when Mr. Carmichael came to Kyrock in 1919 he already had much of the knowledge and experience he needed to make the facility a success.

Mr. Carmichael

Old Hickory Powder Plant Near Nashville, TN

This is a panoramic view of the Old Hickory Powder Plant near Nashville, TN where Mr. Carmichael worked in 1918 prior to being hired to work at Kyrock. The plant was commissioned by the federal government at a cost of 83 million dollars to produce gun powder and explosives for World War I but closed two months after the November 1918 armistice. In 1923 it was purchased by DuPont Corporation who converted it to a rayon factory. In 1924 half of the facility was destroyed by fire consuming 28 million dollars' worth of gunpowder, machinery and buildings.

Chapter 3   Mr. Carmichael

A lot of Harry Carmichael's knowledge about asphalt rock deposits likely came from Colonel Malcolm Hart Crump, a former graduate of his father's alma mater Virginia Military Institute. Colonel Crump was a pioneer in the development of the asphalt rock industry in Edmonson County Kentucky having studied at Harvard about formations of asphalt in the area north of Green River concluding that it could be used for road surfacing thirty years before Harry Carmichael arrived at Kyrock. As a geologist and engineer his contributions in land acquisition, railroad building and his overall knowledge of the geology of the area was unsurpassed.

Colonel Malcolm H. Crump, pioneer of the asphalt industry in Edmonson County Kentucky Oct.14, 1849-Jan. 14, 1925.

DEATH OF COL. MALCOLM H. CRUMP.

Col. Malcolm Hart Crump, one of Kentucky's "Grand Old Men" and a distinguishing engineer and geologist, died in Bowling Green, January 14, from the effects of a stroke of paralysis several months ago.

The news of his death came as a shock to his many friends of long standing in Edmonson county and we shall feel his loss keenly.

Col. Crump was one of the pioneers of the Kentucky rock asphalt field and to him is due much of the credit for its development. As far back as 30 years ago Col. Crump prospected this county thoroughly and for years owned the valuable 3,000-acre tract on which the Kentucky Rock Asphalt company's huge plant is now operating.

Twenty years ago Col. Crump interested capital in the construction of a railroad passing directly through Edmonson county from Bowling Green to the I. C. R. R. Surveys were made, rights of way secured and had it not been for a sudden financial panic throughout the county at that time a railroad for the county seemed assured.

Much of the colonel's time and energies were spent in our neighborhood and even as late as last fall he was instrumental in the sale of a large boundry of asphalt land in the county.

The colonel believed in Edmonson county and loved its people. Nothing pleased him better than to spend a week in the county and merry was the home he stayed in.

Col. Crump was born in Virginia in 1849, was a distinguished graduate of the Virginia Military Institute, class '73, and after working in the engineering department of the B. & O. railroad for a few years he moved to Kentucky.

After teaching school at Hopkinsville for several years he accepted the chair of science in Ogden college and remained there until 20 years ago.

Later he opened an office in Bowling Green as consulting geologist and practiced his profession actively up until the day of his death.

Public spirited to an unusual degree, Col. Crump was a leader in all enterprises for the good of his community and the idea of making money was ever furtherest from his thoughts. It was through his efforts that the street railway was built in Bowling Green, and as engineer for Warren county he did much toward road improvements.

Col. Crump was professionally and socially known throughout the southland and numerous were his friends.

Much to his regret he was too young to enter the services of his beloved southland in the Civil war, but much of his time and talents were devoted to the perpetuation of the ideals of the old south and at the time of his death he was division commander of the state of Kentucky S. C. V.

He was intensely patriotic, of splendid physique and as a soldier was captain of the old Bowling Green Guard and lieutenant-colonel in the Spanish-American war.

He worshipped in the Episcopal church of which he was a constant member.

In fraternal circles he was an Elk, Mason, Kappa Alpha and also belonged to several scientific societies, including Kentucky Academy of Science, Fellow of Royal Society of Arts, XV Club, etc.

A man of splendid Christian character, honest to a fault, a true friend to all mankind and a true exponent of the ideals of the south. His death makes a vacancy that can never be filled, and Edmonson county feels that it has lost a true friend and benefactor. Truly it may be said of him that he lived beyond reproach and died without an enemy.

He is survived by one son, Malcolm H. Crump, Jr., of Bowling Green, to whom the sympathy of Edmonson county is extended.

---o---

Kyrock Personals

Mr. C. P. Moore of Louisville, one of the shining lights in the educational work of the Methodist Church, was in Kyrock for a week during the middle of January. Brother Moore has been engaged for a number of years by the Methodist Church in a work designed to promote and increase the effectiveness of the Sunday school in the religious life of the community. While here he delivered six lectures as part of a course of study leading to that perfect knowledge of child life and human nature which must be the working tools of the really effective Sunday school teacher.

* * *

Miss Sidna Hartzok of Bowling Green paid her farewell visit to Kyrock and spent a week here during the early part of January. She and her brother, Frank Hartzok, are planning to leave the mud roads and hit for the concrete trail in the Keystone state. They will leave Bowling Green during the early part of February and open up a real estate and insurance business in Chambersburg, Pa.

* * *

Mrs. John Causey was hurriedly called to Atlanta, Ga., on account of the serious illness of her father.

* * *

Mr. Albert Porter suffered a temporary attack of blindness that compelled him to seek treatment at the Johns Hopkins hospital, Baltimore, Md.

* * *

While rehearsing for the movies as a daredevil jumper, Mr. Bert Esters miscued and suffered a dislocated knee, which of course is all in the day's work of these movie daredevils.

* * *

Right on scheduled time the cold and lifeless moon attempted to completely hide the bright light from the sun in one of the most spectacular eclipses that has been visible in this country for years. No greater testimony to man's advancement in the knowledge of the great world in which we revolve need be given than that he was able to calculate months in advance the exact minute when the sun's rays would be obscured by the moon, and more intricate yet the exact path of the shadow on the

This page was taken from The Kyrock Messenger (Kyrock Church Publication) published Feb., 1925 in honor of Colonel Malcolm H. Crump who was instrumental in helping to bring the asphalt industry to Edmonson County Kentucky.

Chapter 3   Mr. Carmichael

In 1919 Mr. Carmichael moved his family who consisted of his wife Anna Hetzel, sons Henry St. George Tucker Jr (St. George) and John Randolph Tucker (Ran) and his daughter Anna Hetzel to Kyrock to a modest house near the plant. Since he had no experience in mining asphalt rock he decided to call on some experienced and trusted co-workers from the coal fields where he had built railroads. Among those brought in were John Henrietta, Quarry Superintendent, his brother Charles, Shovel Operator, Lee Percy, Office Manager, Pete Wilson Assistant Office Manager, Jack Johnson, Quarry Superintendent, P. McG. Miller, Civil Engineer and Albert Porter, Night Watchman and Steam Locomotive Maintenance Man. One key to success would be to hire workers who could be trained to operate heavy mining equipment and perform the demanding work necessary to extract the rock asphalt from beneath the earth. The men he initially hired to help start up the new plant would be invaluable in helping train new workers who knew very little about the equipment and procedures used there. Not everyone in the area trusted a mining operation or wanted outsiders coming in making changes to their way of life and it was said that he sometimes had to dodge bullets when driving around in his car after first arriving at the company. One of the first actions taken was to gather all the department heads and quarry superintendents together for a meeting where he vowed to supply them with whatever was needed to make the Kyrock facility successful. The first few months at Kyrock he practically lived in the quarries learning the mining procedures and checking core samples. As new equipment arrived at the plant, more workers were hired and trained. In time people got to know Mr. Carmichael and realized that he wanted what was best for Kyrock and the community. He believed in hard work and demonstrated this by working long hours himself. His day began at 4 AM and usually ended around 7 PM, involving all facets of the plant including mining at the quarry, processing, shipping and one of the areas he thought was extremely important, the Laboratory. Mr. Carmichael realized that the quality of the asphalt rock was a key in the ability to form a tough, durable road surfacing material. He spent much of his time in the Laboratory gaining a thorough understanding of the rock asphalt properties and what was required to make it work best. The rock mined from the quarries needed to have an optimum content of asphalt or bitumen and needed to be kept as clean as possible from dirt or other contaminants. From quarry to final product being loaded for shipment the material had to be checked for bitumen content to meet tight specifications. The strict quality control that Mr. Carmichael demanded was a big reason why the Kyrock plant was successful for so long. But another big reason for the plant's success was the workforce and how Mr. Carmichael interacted with it. The respect and admiration for him inspired the workers to work hard and produce exceptional rock asphalt. When the plant had an exceptional day of production he found ways to demonstrate his appreciation like blowing the plant whistle long and loud. Slowly but surely the Kyrock plant began to reap the reward of all the hard work to become a successful and profitable operation. Mr. Carmichael did not concentrate his efforts only on the Kyrock plant, but he also understood and provided for the needs of the Kyrock community. Emphasis on education was a priority and one of the first construction projects was building the Kyrock School.

Shortly after moving to Kyrock tragedy struck the Carmichael family when wife Anna died in 1920 leaving Mr. Carmichael with two young sons and daughter ages thirteen, ten and five to attend to as well as getting the new Kyrock operation started. It must have taken a great deal of time and energy to see to all the needs of the company and his family. In 1921 a young lady by the name of Lalla Stanrod came from Rockcastle, Kentucky in Trigg County to teach at the Kyrock School. She lived for a while in the Log Hotel in the Kyrock Woodside community and immediately caught the eye of Mr. Carmichael. He was immediately smitten by her and thus began a courtship which resulted in their marriage in 1921. It seemed that the Carmichaels might finally be settling into their new family arrangement with Lalla now helping to raise the three children and Mr. Carmichael working long hours at Kyrock. The two older boys attended the Kyrock School for a while prior to going on to the Ogden Prep School in Bowling Green, Kentucky. In 1923 tragedy struck again when little nine-year old Anna became gravely ill with diphtheria and died from complications of pneumonia. While attending to the many problems of running a large mining and processing operation, he also had to deal with his daughter's death. The next year, however, good fortune came when Lalla gave birth to their son Stanrod. In 1928 more good fortune came when Johnny was born into the Carmichael home. The same year as baby Johnny was being prepared to be brought to the Kyrock house it burned and a new house that still stands today had to be built. The new house was much bigger and better than the original one. It had a basement, main floor with large screened porch and an upstairs. The Carmichael boys attended Kyrock School for a while and after 1934 began school in Bowling Green, Kentucky. For a while the family lived in a furnished apartment there during winter while the boys attended school and Mr. Carmichael commuted back and forth to Kyrock. Eventually the family bought a house on Chestnut Street in Bowling Green in 1936 and began spending winters there and summers at the Kyrock house. Lalla Carmichael disliked her virtual social isolation at Kyrock and enjoyed the social life in Bowling Green. Being the superintendent's wife at Kyrock could be difficult but Lalla and Harry did their best to make the house at Kyrock a happy home.

Mr. Carmichael

This is believed to be a photo of Stan and his mother Lalla when baby Johnny was being brought from Bowling Green, Ky. His arrival to Kyrock had to be delayed until the new house could be built, since the one they had been living in unexpectedly burned soon after his birth.

Young Stanrod gazed at his new brother Johnny at their new home in Kyrock in 1928.

Stan commented that Johnny wasn't much fun to play with until he was about four years old. When Johnny grew older the two were pretty much inseparable on the 30 acre Kyrock estate where their house was located. The boys moved to Bowling Green, KY to attend school after Stan finished 5th grade in 1934. Weekends and summer months were spent at Kyrock thereafter.

Chapter 3 **Mr. Carmichael**

This is a photo of the Carmichael house taken not long after it was built. Note that on the left side on top of the hill you can see the back side of the Kyrock Church.

This photo shows Johnny giving his dog Jodus a long stare. Stan recalled that at an early age Johnny developed his own language for all the dogs at Kyrock that only the dogs could understand.

This photo was taken sometime around 1930 showing members of the Carmichael family beginning left to right with Stanrod, Lalla, Johnny, Harry, Unknown and St. George. The other brother Randolph (Ran) is not shown.

Chapter 3 Mr. Carmichael

Stan and Johnny along with dog Jodus stand outside the new house that was built for the Carmichael family when the original one burned after Johnny was born in 1928.

This is a photo of the Carmichael house located at 1220 State Street in Bowling Green, KY. The Carmichael family began living here about 1936, while spending summers and weekends at Kyrock.

Chapter 3   Mr. Carmichael

Mr. Carmichael routinely brought in African American workers to serve as cooks, maids and handymen around the Carmichael residence. They lived in residences located on the Carmichael estate at Kyrock. Johnny and Stan are being watched by these workers in this photo.

Stanrod recalled that as many as seven African American men, women and children were brought in to help at the Carmichael house to work as cooks, maids and handymen. Their presence there was not kept secret or publicized to local residents although most were aware that they worked for Mr. Carmichael. These workers either stayed in houses near the Carmichael residence or in the Carmichael house. There were never any objections reported from their presence in the community even though there were no other African Americans who lived within twenty five miles of Kyrock. Stanrod stated that his favorite friend was an African American from Bowling Green who spent considerable time at Kyrock.

Mr. Carmichael

This is a photo of Johnny and Stan along with their mother Lalla near the office building at Kyrock taken about the mid-1930's.

Chapter 3   Mr. Carmichael

Stanrod and Johnny had many fond memories of their time at Kyrock. Their years at Kyrock School were challenging but exciting times. They played baseball and all kinds of children's activities like marbles, fox and hound, cowboys and Indians and anything their imagination could invent. There were times when they rode around the property on Johnny's paint pony Joe de Soto or played in the shallow cement lined swimming pool near the woods just 250 or so yards from the house.

These photos show Johnny and Stan riding Johnny's paint pony Joe Desoto around the Carmichael property

Mr. Carmichael

Johnny and Stan Carmichael always enjoyed playing cowboys and Indians as well as other games with the local boys during their times at Kyrock.

This is a photo of Stan and Johnny along with a friend taking a swim in what is believed to be the cement lined swimming pool near their house.

Chapter 3   Mr. Carmichael

Stan and Johnny along with a playmate posed for a photo just outside the back porch where they always had plenty of animals available for company.

They sometimes spent time building crude airplanes from the empty dynamite boxes or scraping out roads for their cars made from mason jars or tin cans. Stan was more of the bookworm whereas Johnny was the outdoorsman of the two. Stan could lose himself in the thousand volume library in the Carmichael house while Johnny was usually outside with his menagerie of dogs and other animals that wandered freely around the property.

A story relayed by Mr. Carmichael's son Johnny as well as some of the former Kyrock workers illustrated his love for animals. A quail had built a nest in one of the Kyrock quarries that was being prepared to open for mining. When Mr. Carmichael was informed of the presence of the nest he instructed the workers to hold off opening the quarry until the young quails chicks had left the nest. He was also an avid hunter and sportsman. His fondness for animals was obvious when

Mr. Carmichael

In this photo Stan (In the center) posed with some of his friends while Johnny holds the reigns to a sheep pulling a "Blue Grass Farm Wagon". There was never a shortage of animals around the house to help entertain the boys. Note the snow sled next to the house. The names of the other boys are unknown but likely are visitors to the Carmichael house.

As this photo shows there were always plenty of dogs around at the Carmichael home in Kyrock to keep Johnny and Stan preoccupied. At one time there may have been as many as 27 dogs there along with other animals.

you approached his house at Kyrock. At one time it was said that he owned 27 dogs of various breeds including Great Danes, Saint Bernards, Dachshunds and Cocker Spaniels. Dogs as well as game chickens, fighting cocks, African geese or goats often greeted visitors to the house. Mr. Carmichael's daughter in-law once made the comment after a visit to the house that it was like "opening the door to a zoo".

This photo was taken on a cold winter day when Johnny and Stan were standing on frozen water. The young man with them may have been one of their older step brothers from Mr. Carmichael's first wife Anna. The older gentleman is unknown. As always there were always some friendly dogs along to keep them company.

Chapter 3   Mr. Carmichael

This photo is one of Stan Carmichael posing near the Kyrock High School (Note the basketball goal) with one of the popular homemade toys at Kyrock, a metal wheel rolled along the ground using a specially made stick with a metal guide at the bottom. Children would play with these for hours to entertain themselves.

Mr. Carmichael

This is a photo taken aboard Miss Nolin steam boat docked at Kyrock in 1938. It was taken at the same time as the one in Social Life and Entertainment. In the photo from left to right seated are Boadley Davenport, Sheriff of Warren County; Harry St. George Tucker Carmichael, Kyrock Superintendent; Governor A.B. (Happy) Chandler; Alton B. Mitchell, representative of Edmonson and Butler Counties; Robert Humphrey; Standing are Emory G. Dent, Bowling Green, Kentucky Highway Commissioner; William H. Natcher, Warren County Attorney; Cecil Williams, Somerset member of Kentucky Highway Commission. Mr. Natcher later represented Kentucky as U.S. Representative from 1953 until his death in 1994.

Johnnie Carmichael said that his dad could fraternize with kings or paupers. He had many friends and acquaintances among them being bureaucrats and politicians. Many of these people were anxious to have their pictures taken with the superintendent of one on the most productive manufacturing facilities in the state.

Chapter 3   Mr. Carmichael

In January 1925 Harry Carmichael gained notoriety from an incident near Mammoth Cave Kentucky where Floyd Collins, a local cave explorer, became trapped in Sand Cave. Mr. Carmichael was called in to help dig a tunnel to help rescue Floyd Collins. After weeks of delay before the tunnel could be approved and numerous problems encountered in digging the tunnel the famous cave explorer perished before he could be freed. Mr. Carmichael had supplied not only his own time and hard work but also provided Kyrock workers and supplies to the endeavor.

Photo of Mr. & Mrs. H. T. Carmichael taken by a reporter in February, 1925. They are standing near Sand Cave which is now located inside Mammoth Cave National Park. Mr. H.T. Carmichael and his workers from the Kyrock Asphalt Company had been asked to do excavation work in hopes of reaching the trapped Floyd Collins.

37

THE ALUMNI MAGAZINE   11

H. T. Carmichael, '99 --- Humanitarian

Never has the fate of one unknown and obscure human being caught the interest and sympathy of a whole nation as did the entombment of Floyd Collins at Sand Cave, Kentucky. The very spirit of human brotherhood was plumbed and proven in the heroic attempts to rescue this Kentucky mountaineer from his rock-barred tomb.

Calmly and tirelessly directing the rescue work stood the figure of H. T. Carmichael, '99, the incarnation of that spirit of human brotherhood—a spirit reflected in every move of the straining workers below. Mr. Carmichael's account of the work at Sand Cave is told in the terse, graphic sentences of an engineer on the opposite page.

An editorial in the Nashville Banner said:

"A month ago the friends of H. T. Carmichael of Kyrock, Kentucky, were, to all intents and purposes, limited to the number of individuals who had come in personal contact with him in his career as a successful engineer. Then there came to him a call to lend a hand in the rescue of a man he did not know, trapped in a crumbling passageway in the cave country. It was not long before Carmichael of Kyrock was in command. The crews of volunteer workers quickly learned to respect his leadership even though the way led into the tottering depths of a rotten hillside."

A news report in the Louisville (Kentucky) Courier-Journal said:

"Directing and planning continuously day and night, driving brain and body almost to the snapping point, yet never flustered, Mr. Carmichael moved back and forth through the scene, always leaving reassurance in his wake where before there had been doubt and often almost despair.

"It was an eloquent picture of service for others, thrown for a brief period by the hand of providence perhaps upon the screen of everyday life, for what is supposed to be a world run mad with selfish and mercenary impulses, and the world rose to the picture with uncovered heads and beating hearts.

"'If your faith in humanity ever falters,' Mr. Carmichael told Lee Collins when the task of the shaft-diggers was ended, 'just remember that there are those whose faith extends to all parts of the earth.'"

The Cleveland (Ohio) Plain Dealer said:

"We shall remember Carmichael, the engineer. He knew where to sink the shaft, he knew how to sink it. He knew how to keep the men intelligently employed. He spared himself not at all, but worked with them and encouraged them by example as well as by skillful direction. Carmichael will not be forgotten."

H. St. George Tucker Carmichael, '99

Thus the world acclaimed the efforts of Mr. Carmichael and his men.

Harry Tucker Carmichael is the grandson of the Honorable John Randolph Tucker, former dean of the Washington and Lee law school, and the nephew of the Honorable Harry St. George Tucker, '76 Congressman from Virginia. He lived in Lexington with his parents, Captain and Mrs. John Carmichael, until his graduation from the engineering school of W. and L. in 1890.

Since graduation his life has been that of his profession, living from pillar to post in various railroad construction camps until 1920 when he became general superintendent for the Kentucky Rock Asphalt Company at Kyrock, Kentucky. As engineer in charge of railroad construction and location he was active in building the lines of the B. and O. Railway, the C. and O., the Western Maryland, and the C. C. and O. During the war he superintended the construction and grading of eight miles of track at the Old Hickory powder plant. The line was ready for operation in thirty days, which is considered a world's record for such work.

Mr. Carmichael is a member of the Kappa Alpha fraternity, the B. P. O. E., the Kentucky Academy of Science, and a fellow of the Royal Society for the Encouragement of Arts, Manufacture and Commerce, London, England.

This 1925 article in the Washington and Lee Alumni Magazine describes Mr. Carmichael's involvement in the Floyd Collins rescue attempt at Sand Cave near Mammoth Cave, Kentucky.

Chapter 3　　Mr. Carmichael

Mr. Carmichael demonstrated his support of Kyrock School by sometimes visiting the school, or dropping in at sporting events, especially baseball games. He could sometimes be seen picking up people for a ride to the school.

This photo of his dad when he was a young man playing baseball for The Maryland Masonic Baseball Team was a prized possession of Stan Carmichael. He proudly displayed it in his living room and shared this copy with me just before he passed away. Mr. Carmichael was an enthusiastic fan of baseball and when he became superintendent at Kyrock he established a semi-professional team at the plant and promoted school teams as well as summer baseball teams.

Chapter 3   Mr. Carmichael

Being an avid baseball fan he actively promoted the sport at Kyrock. He helped establish a semi-professional team at Kyrock that was competitive throughout the state. It was a common practice to find jobs for those who showed superior baseball skills. A story told by his son Stanrod described an incident when young Harry St. George Tucker Carmichael who was nicknamed "Whitey" for his premature white-blond hair was playing on a baseball team where he was an especially talented pitcher. During one of his games he was so confident in his pitching ability that he instructed all the outfielders to come in and watch him pitch while he retired the opposing batters. He passed along his passion and love for the sport at Kyrock. Kyrock School seemed to always have one on the best teams in the region and the "pro" team served as entertainment for the community. Stanrod and Johnny grew to love baseball and took advantage of every opportunity to play at Kyrock.

Mr. Carmichael was a compassionate man with a kind spirit. His son Stan Carmichael recalled that when baby brother Johnnie slept in his mother's bedroom he and his father would share the other bedroom. Each night before going to bed his dad would bow on his knees to pray making an indelible impression on Stan. He described his father as a compassionate and good man. Once when Mr. Carmichael was driving back from Lexington, Virginia in his 1928 Studebaker he saw a man along the side of the road and as he was usually prone to do he stopped and gave the man a ride to Bowling Green. Afterwards, he discovered that the man had stolen all of his money. The police were informed of the theft and apprehended the man who was put in jail. Mr. Carmichael was so troubled that the man had been put in jail that he went to visit him and took him some candy and magazines to pass the time.

Mr. Carmichael

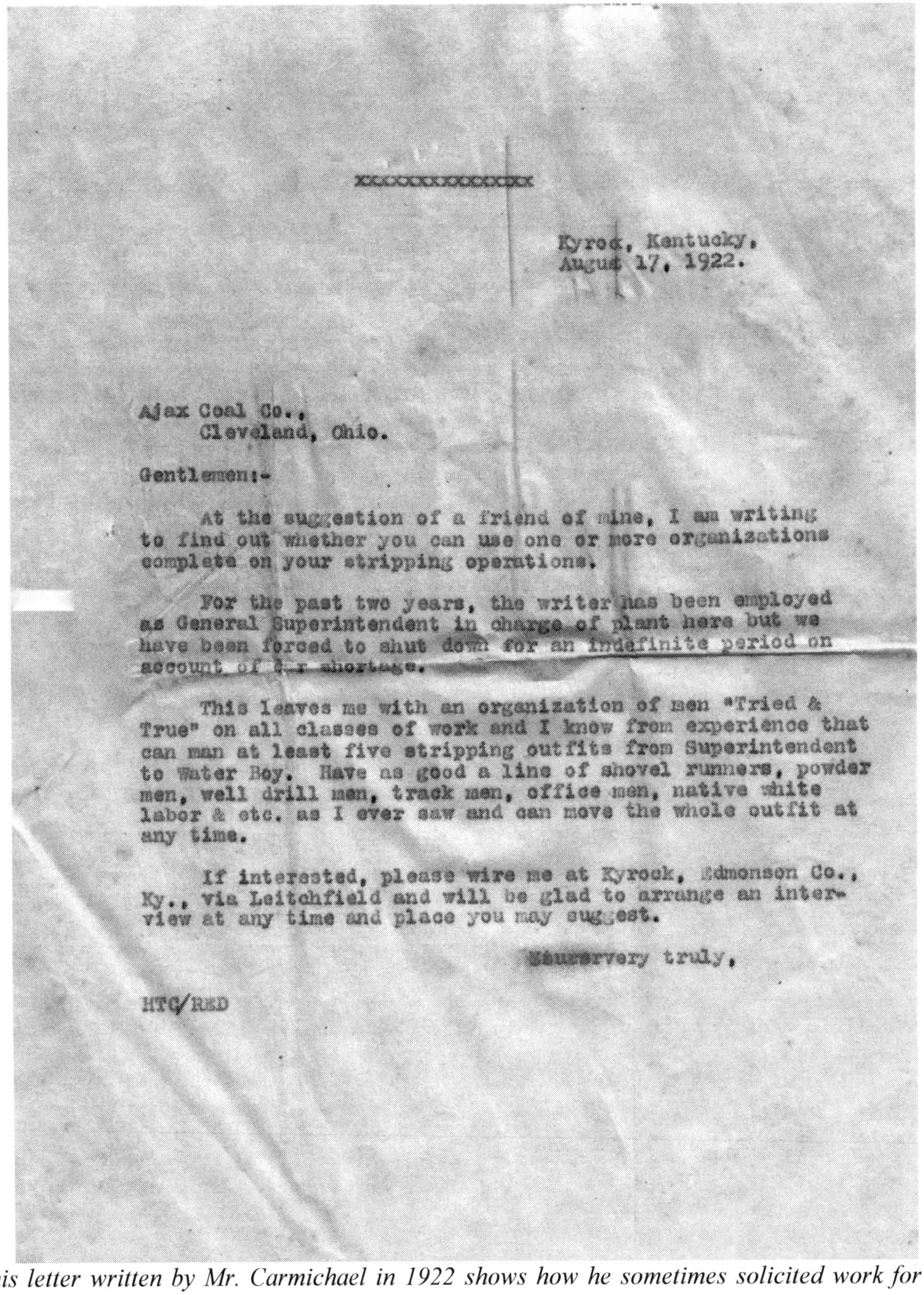

XXXXXXXXXXXXXXX

Kyrock, Kentucky,
August 17, 1922.

Ajax Coal Co.,
Cleveland, Ohio.

Gentlemen:-

At the suggestion of a friend of mine, I am writing to find out whether you can use one or more organizations complete on your stripping operations.

For the past two years, the writer has been employed as General Superintendent in charge of plant here but we have been forced to shut down for an indefinite period on account of car shortage.

This leaves me with an organization of men "Tried & True" on all classes of work and I know from experience that can man at least five stripping outfits from Superintendent to Water Boy. Have as good a line of shovel runners, powder men, well drill men, track men, office men, native white labor & etc. as I ever saw and can move the whole outfit at any time.

If interested, please wire me at Kyrock, Edmonson Co., Ky., via Leitchfield and will be glad to arrange an interview at any time and place you may suggest.

Yours very truly,

HTC/RED

This letter written by Mr. Carmichael in 1922 shows how he sometimes solicited work for his employees when times were slow at the Kyrock plant.

Chapter 3   Mr. Carmichael

Harry St. James Tucker Carmichael preferred to be called Harry but nearly everyone at Kyrock called him Mr. Carmichael out of respect and admiration. He served as superintendent of Kentucky Rock Asphalt Company from 1919 until 1949.

Chapter 3   Mr. Carmichael

In the early years of Kyrock the needs of the area were many. There were no doctors or dentists nearby and supplies were scarce. There were few houses and most residents in the area "got by" from raising their own food. After Mr. Carmichael arrived he helped provide some of the basic necessities. The company built houses for workers who didn't have one. A doctor was brought in to attend not only Kyrock workers, but also other members of the community. There was even a small hospital for emergencies. Dental care was provided and a barber shop was available. Commissaries carried food and supplies at reasonable prices.

During the years of the great depression Kyrock workers were sometimes paid scrip to be spent at the Commissary. Mr. Carmichael sometimes solicited work outside the Kyrock facility to keep his employees working as much as possible. He headed the state organization to fight infantile paralysis in Kentucky and was active in other worthwhile charitable causes. Social activities like Chautauqua, outdoor plays, movies, baseball games, and basketball tournaments were held. There were Christmas and 4th of July celebrations. Mr. Carmichael supported these activities because he realized that these things were necessary for the community. It is impossible to name all the contributions he made to the community while he was superintendent at Kyrock.

Chapter 4 Quarry and Mining Operations

The first quarry to open at Kyrock was Quarry No. 1 later referred to as "the old quarry" was located on the top of the hill near the plant. At least eight were opened near the plant. Later six additional quarries were opened farther from the plant as there was more demand for rock asphalt. These quarries were called Morris, Pine Creek, Indian Creek, Sweeden, Beaver Dam and Black Gold.

Gaining access to the rich deposits of rock asphalt required the use of strip mining techniques to remove the layer of "overburden" consisting of dirt, shale and stone. This layer could be as thick as forty feet or more. To get to the rock asphalt layer the workers would remove the layer of overburden using various techniques. To determine how much of the layer needed to be removed a series of holes were drilled using a core driller. If the layer was less than six feet workers would use a

Kyrock Core Drillers: Morris Webb on left along with his brother Walter Webb (center) and Walter's son , J.C. on the right. Morris and Walter worked side by side from the early 1930's through the early 1950's. When Walter retired, Morris continued working for Kyrock until they closed in the late 1950's. The core drillers moved from place to place taking sample core to see where asphalt was located. The drills that were used were operated by using black diamond bits. The black diamonds were set in the bits by hand.

44

Chapter 4 Quarry and Mining Operations

Workers clearing overburden using high pressure water piped from the Nolin River. This method was only used for a short time at Kyrock.

high pressure sprayer with 160 psi capacity with water pumped from the Nolin River to remove the top layer. If the layer was thicker than about six feet it had to be removed by steam shovels. Use of high pressure sprayers was abandoned eventually. Many operations relied heavily on manual labor that could be very difficult and hazardous. Sometimes holes were drilled in the overburden and packed with dynamite. As much as nine cases of dynamite could be placed in one hole with

Chapter 4 Quarry and Mining Operations

a hole about every 12 to 14 feet apart as many as fifty holes at the site. Sometimes pieces of the dynamite did not explode and became mixed in with the overburden. One story was told by Walter Gipson, a former steam shovel operator at Kyrock, about how he once started removing overburden and dug out some of the dynamite. He notified his supervisor who brought in a group of workers with picks and shovels to dig out three or four cases of unexploded dynamite.

In this photo a steam powered shovel is clearing and loading overburden into wagons transported on rails to the nearest dump area. These giant shovels had to be used when needed to remove thick layers of dirt, rocks and other debris to reach the deposits of asphalt rock.

Chapter 4 Quarry and Mining Operations

In this photo workers can be seen cleaning asphalt rock (on left) in preparation for breaking it up with dynamite. A steam shovel is working nearby and what appears to be a core driller is on top of the hill above along with a water tank on the right side. Water had to be pumped to the quarries for use in steam powered equipment.

After the overburden was removed it was loaded into road wagons or later into small railroad carts and transported to the nearest dump area. The surface of the rock asphalt was cleaned to remove any dirt or debris using either high pressure water or merely swept clean with brooms. When it was clean, air drills were used to drill 4 inch holes for dynamite, as many as sixteen sticks, which was then exploded to break the rock into pieces that could be either broken up by hand with picks or hammers or small enough to be loaded into skip boxes.

Chapter 4 Quarry and Mining Operations

A steam shovel clears overburden and loads it in a nearby rail car.

Like the dynamite used on overburden it could also sometimes go unexploded and had to be dug out by workers. If a rock was too large to be broken up by workers it had to be shot again to break it into smaller pieces.

From the beginning of the Kyrock Plant the mining and processing steps were continually undergoing improvements to reduce labor requirements and improve efficiency. Prior to 1922 when a larger new crusher was installed rock asphalt had to be manually reduced to a size small enough to be dumped into a 22 inch by 50 inch crusher. A substantial amount of manual labor was needed for this job requiring as many as 400 men per day to break up the asphalt rock into pieces small enough to be loaded into the smaller crusher. During this time period asphalt

Chapter 4 **Quarry and Mining Operations**

Workmen at the Quarry breaking up asphalt rock in preparation of loading into skip boxes or rail wagons and transporting it on the nearby tracks to the Crusher. Air drill marks can be seen on the nearby rock where dynamite had been placed for exploding. Experienced workmen were trained to select rock asphalt with just the right amount of asphalt content to meet specifications.

Chapter 4 **Quarry and Mining Operations**

Workers in this photo are sorting and loading asphalt rock into skip boxes at Quarry #1. Nearby is a steam powered crane that likely lifted the boxes up for loading into rail wagons that transported it to the crusher. In the upper part of the photo there appears to be a steam operated shovel clearing away debris. (Photo from collection of Mary Gladys Vincent Kinser whose father operated a steam shovel from 1919 until Kyrock was closed.

rock was loaded by hand into skip boxes and road wagons and brought to the top of the hill where they were emptied into one of two giant buckets referred to as "Gongs". These buckets moved on a railroad track and were pulled by cables that carried them along the hillside approximately 300 yards. When a loaded bucket descended to the plant and was dumped into what was called the "bull pen" the other empty one was refilled and the process repeated. After the large crusher was installed a system of rail lines were built from the quarries to the plant and a fleet of "dinkeys" or small locomotives fueled by coal that ran on steam fired 18 ton engines running at about 140 psi were used to pull 10 to 12 rail cars of asphalt rock to the crusher.

In this photo workers at Quarry #2 are loading asphalt rock into skip boxes where a nearby steam powered crane picks them up and transfers them to rail wagons. On the hill above is a steam powered shovel clearing debris. A dinkey sets on the tracks preparing to transport the asphalt rock to the crusher.

Chapter 4 **Quarry and Mining Operations**

In this photo workmen at Quarry #9 are breaking up asphalt rocks and loading into open ended boxes that will be picked up by a crane and dumped into rail car wagons. The asphalt rock in these wagons were then transported to the plant for crushing.

After the large crusher was put into operation the mining process became more efficient since pieces of asphalt rock as large as 4 feet by 4 feet could the brought to the plant with less manual labor needed to break up the rocks. Workers cleaned off dirt and debris from the asphalt rock before blasting and then used jackhammers to reduce the blasted rocks to 4 foot square or less if needed.

Chapter 4 Quarry and Mining Operations

In this photo a steam shovel appears to be loading rail cars with asphalt rock while a dinkey prepares to move them to the plant for crushing. To the right can be seen where overburden has been dumped on the hillside and track has been laid nearby it. Workers are sorting through rocks at various locations to find those suitable for loading. Crews of men were always kept busy moving tracks or building new ones for the dinkeys.

Chapter 4 **Quarry and Mining Operations**

These Kyrock workers are standing on a large piece of asphalt rock at the Indian Creek Quarry likely preparing it for dynamite blasting. The steam shovel on the left side of the photo appears to be cleaning off dirt and debris from the area.

The large chunks of rock were then loaded onto four-ten (4 feet by ten feet) rail cars called "Four Yarders" using either a steam shovel or a derrick. Derricks were stationery upright masts with turning circular bases and had a boom. At the top of the boom was a cable with hooks that could be extended downward to pick up rocks as heavy as four to five tons. Workers had to move the derricks closer to new piles of asphalt rock as the older sections were mined away. Workers were usually anxious to learn how to operate derricks and other types of large equipment because the wages were better and the work was not as strenuous.

Chapter 4 Quarry and Mining Operations

In this photo a derrick is loading large pieces of asphalt rock into a rail car. The derrick could be moved by rail to new sites when an existing site became depleted of suitable asphalt rock with acceptable bitumen content.

The use of dinkeys, which were basically just small steam powered locomotives, increased as time passed with higher production rates and quarries located farther from the processing plant. About two dinkeys were added to the fleet each year until it reached 21. The dinkeys could pull 10 to 12 cars loaded with asphalt rock headed to the crusher. They could also pull loads of overburden to dump sites when new deposits of asphalt rock were being mined.

Chapter 4 **Quarry and Mining Operations**

In the photo above Kyrock Dinkey Operator Pete Decker shows off Dinkey No. 219 which he called "Old 19" as it appeared in 1925 when he was only 26 years old.

In this photo Kyrock Asphalt Co. showed off the 17 locomotives the company owned at the time.

Chapter 4 Quarry and Mining Operations

In this 1929 photo a dinkey in the center of the photo returns to the quarry for another load of asphalt rock while a steam shovel works nearly hidden below a cliff excavating another area. On the hill above a crew works with a core driller taking core samples.

With the addition of more dinkeys and the opening of more quarries workmen were kept busy repairing or removing old track lines and laying down new ones. In addition, some of the steam shovels and dump wagons had to run on the tracks. With quarries as far as eight miles away from the plant the number of track lines to build and maintain was substantial.

Chapter 4 **Quarry and Mining Operations**

In the photo above newly laid track can be seen as a nearby steam shovel sits by probably used to help workmen in the job. In the background another steam shovel can also be seen.

In addition to strip mining, early mining practices also included digging tunnels as far as several hundred feet horizontally into the veins of asphalt rock. It was then loaded into rail cars and transported to the crusher. The rails did not extend very far into the tunnels necessitating it to be transported by hand to the rail cars. Workers usually exited these tunnels soaked with water and sweat. This method of mining eliminated having to remove the overburden layer but the method was abandoned probably because it became difficult to remove the large asphalt rocks from inside the tunnels and possibly because of the danger of cave ins inside the tunnels.

Chapter 4 **Quarry and Mining Operations**

The photos below illustrated how the tunnels at Kyrock were constructed and mined. Once a vein of asphalt rock was located workers blasted and dug a tunnel horizontally into the hillside collecting rock as they worked. These rocks were loaded into boxes and transported by rail to the crusher.

In this photo workers are just starting to dig a new tunnel. The next photos show their progress as new tunnels are excavated and tracks are laid to the new ones.

Chapter 4 Quarry and Mining Operations

Chapter 4 Quarry and Mining Operations

Chapter 4   Quarry and Mining Operations

Chapter 4   Quarry and Mining Operations

Chapter 4 **Quarry and Mining Operations**

This is a photo showing how the tunnels at the Indian Creek Quarry appeared about 1937. This method of mining was used for a time at Kyrock to remove asphalt rock but the procedure was later abandoned.

Throughout the years mining methods at Kyrock evolved as technology and procedures improved. Eventually the use of dinkeys was replaced with trucks to haul the rocks to the crusher. Equipment was modernized by replacing steam powered equipment with gasoline or diesel powered equipment but the work remained labor intensive for mining the asphalt rocks.

Chapter 5   Processing and Shipping

When processing operations first began at the Kyrock Plant sometime around 1918 asphalt rock from the quarry was brought to the processing area in skip boxes or road wagons from which it had to be removed by hand and placed in one of two giant buckets. The buckets ran on a double railroad track and were pulled by cables that ran approximately three hundred yards down the hillside. As the filled bucket was lowered to the plant the empty bucket was forced up the hill to be re-filled. Each time the filled bucket descended to the plant it was emptied into what was called the "bullpen" which was a 1000 ton storage bin. The bullpen had

This photo is believed to show the first method for moving loads of rock asphalt to the smaller crusher prior to installation of the large crusher. Note the old wooden water tank next to the building as well as the commissary. At the left center there are several buildings including the Blue Town Hotel. All appear only to have been recently built.

Chapter 5   Processing and Shipping

various compartments each with different grades of asphalt rock from various locations or quarries and each with known amounts of bitumen (asphalt) content. This arrangement allowed higher or lower bitumen content rock to be released from the bullpen through a series of gates to insure the correct amount of bitumen content in the finished product. Downstream from the crushing and milling process samples were taken to the laboratory and tested for bitumen content. If adjustments needed to be made on the discharge gates this could be done to obtain the correct bitumen content.

This is the Belt Conveyor from Crusher to Bin at the Kyrock Asphalt Company. The structure is still under construction with no siding on the outside frame walls. Photo was taken by Borst Photo around the early 1920's.

Around 1922 the company obtained a large 60"x48" crusher that could accommodate asphalt rock as large as four feet square. This crusher could reduce the asphalt rock to seven inches and under. The crushed rock could then be fed onto a thirty-inch belt conveyor which transported it to the bullpen. Prior to the installation of the larger crusher and the belt conveyor asphalt rocks had been transported to the smaller crusher using giant buckets. This made a significant impact on the mining and processing steps increasing efficiency and reducing manual labor.

Chapter 5   Processing and Shipping

This is a photo of the large 60"x48" crusher that was installed in 1922-1923 at the Kyrock Plant. This crusher could reduce the size of asphalt rock as large as four feet to pieces seven inches or smaller having a significant impact on labor and efficiency.

Around the time the large crusher was installed the plant began expanding its fleet of dinkeys. Smaller dinkeys were used to transport asphalt rock from the quarry to the "main line" rail. The larger dinkeys, called "main line dinkeys", were coupled to 10-12 of the rail cars which then pulled the cars to the large crusher. The asphalt was then loaded into the large crusher where it was reduced to a size seven inches or smaller. These pieces then traveled about 130 feet down the thirty-inch conveyor belt to the bullpen and then to the smaller 22"x50" crusher.

Chapter 5 Processing and Shipping

In this photo a dinkey delivers a load of asphalt rock to the building containing the large crusher. Dinkeys could usually pull about 10-12 rail cars of rock on the "main line".

In this photo a dinkey can be seen returning empty rail cars after a trip to the large crusher.

Chapter 5   Processing and Shipping

In this photo asphalt rock is being transferred on a conveyor from the large primary crusher to the bullpen where it was mixed with rock from various locations before being transferred to the smaller crusher.

After the asphalt rock passed through the small crusher the pieces were no larger than about four inches. These pieces were discharged into a rotary screen with two inch openings. The oversize pieces went to a fifty-two inch crushing roll which reduced it to 1 ½ -inch maximum size and subsequently onto a series of three belt conveyors which fed six 42"x16" smooth rolls. The material passing through a revolving screen was discharged directly onto the same conveyors. The smooth crushing rolls pulverized the pieces to a size about the same as coarse sand. Eventually the rollers were replaced with a system called a "hammer mill".

Chapter 5 **Processing and Shipping**

This is an early photo of the processing plant at Kyrock. Note that the sides have not been closed in and rail lines were being used to transport wagons down the hill. Workers filled the empty wagons with railroad ties they had hewn before returning them. It is believed this photo was taken around the time the plant was changing from use of buckets to fill barges to a conveyor system.

At this point in the process a dipper sample of crushed stone was taken for the laboratory to test for bitumen content. If the sample was too lean or too high the gates on the bullpen had to be adjusted to let rock asphalt with either higher or lower bitumen content through so that the finished material met the required specification. In this way the material was always under strict process control. Prior to the construction of the Kyrock Canal a system of buckets or wagons were used to carry the finished rock asphalt to a barge on the Nolin River.

Chapter 5   Processing and Shipping

This is a birds-eye view of the old processing building prior to building the new Kyrock Harbor and the conveyor system to load finished product into the barges. Notice on the right side of this photo can be seen the commissary as well as the building and screen used to watch movies.

At that time the finished product was discharged into a chute which was used to fill one of six one-ton buckets. The buckets were attached to a cable which ran in a circle from the chute used to fill the buckets to the barges on Nolin River. A worker guided the filled bucket or later a wagon to the barge and emptied it into the barge. After wagons were emptied they were filled with railroad ties that were hewn by the workers and returned up the hill eventually to the quarry.

About the time the large crusher was installed at the top of the hill a construction crew from Muscle Shoals, Alabama was brought in to the plant to build a new

Chapter 5   Processing and Shipping

This photo shows how Kyrock Landing on the Nolin River appeared before the construction of the loading facility on the newly built Kyrock Harbor. Barges are lined up and being filled while a steam boat prepares to pull them down the river and eventually to the distribution facility.

conveyor and chute from the processing plant to a new canal being built from No-lin River. The new 216-foot conveyor and chute led directly over the canal where barges could be loaded without the use of the bucket system. Within this conveyor was a "weightometer" which automatically recorded the tonnage delivered to the barges while a sampling device under the conveyor collected samples for testing. These were examples of how improvements were constantly being made at Kyrock to make it more efficient, safer and less dependent on manual labor. Prior to construction of Kyrock Harbor more time and manual labor was required to load the barges by filling the large buckets or wagons. After being thoroughly mixed and tested during processing the rock asphalt finished product was loaded onto barges for transport to the distribution facility.

Chapter 5   Processing and Shipping

This is a photo of the processing plant at Kyrock after the building was closed in and a conveyor was built. The Kyrock Canal was in the process of being built. Notice the new water tank on the hill.

Picture shows the loading of asphalt on the barges in the Kyrock Asphalt Company's canal. Notice the steamboat in the canal. The pipeline in the foreground carried steam up the hill to some of the homes on top. The picture was taken by Borst Photo around the early 1920's.

Photo from Pictorial History of Edmonson County

Chapter 5   Processing and Shipping

In this photo finished rock asphalt product is being loaded into barges using the new conveyor and chute built over Kyrock Harbor.

Until the mid-1940's the lack of accessibility of the plant by rail or truck required that all shipments be made by barges being pulled up the Nolin, Green and Barren Rivers. The barges were built by a crew of African American men and were twenty six feet wide by one-hundred feet long carrying three-hundred tons each. Sternwheel steamboats were used to pull the barges a distance of about seventy miles to Bowling Green, Kentucky taking around eighteen hours. The return trip to the plant took about twice as long due to upstream currents, even while carrying a lighter load of coal and other supplies back to the plant.

Chapter 5   Processing and Shipping

Kyrock Processing

Quarry

Crushing Mill

Conveyor

Secondary Crusher

Finishing Mills

Kyrock Harbor

Nolin River

This photograph shows the entire process of preparing rock asphalt as a finished product beginning with large boulders from the Quarry and ending with a finished product that was approximately the consistency of sand. The nearby Nolin River was then utilized by loading barges with the product at Kyrock Harbor and pulling them down the river by steam boat to the distribution center.

Processing and Shipping

This is a photo of a recently built barge being launched at Kyrock. These barges were loaded with finished asphalt rock and pulled by steamboat to the distribution facility.

In this photo a steam boat is pulling two barges fully loaded with finished Kyrock product.

Chapter 5   Processing and Shipping

Many of the supplies including coal were brought in by steamboat to Kyrock. This was the cheapest and most efficient method of moving materials.

This photo shows the coal hoist used to unload coal from barges during early days of Kyrock.

This is a picture of the General Logan steamboat pushing a barge in the Kyrock Asphalt Company's canal. The steamboats would push the barges full of asphalt to the storage yard in Bowling Green and then would push barges full of coal back to the Asphalt Company. This picture was taken by Borst Photo around the early 1920's.

This photo shows an old stern wheeler pulling a barge of Kyrock product to a distribution facility in Bowling Green, Kentucky or Rockport, Kentucky.

Chapter 5   Processing and Shipping

The Betty Turner Steamboat pulled the next to last barge of Kyrock asphalt and the New Hanover Steamboat pulled the final barge in October, 1946. The boats were owned by Thomas W. Hines and James R. Hines. Thereafter the material was trucked to distribution points.

Chapter 5 **Processing and Shipping**

Kentucky Rock Asphalt being unloaded from barges at the Bowling Green, Kentucky distribution Center.

Some of the shipments were made to another distribution point eighty miles down the Green River to Rockport, Kentucky for shipment by the Illinois Central Rail Road rather than the Louisville Nashville Rail Road. A series of locks and dams on the rivers assured a fairly constant water level and the US government assisted keeping the waterways navigable insuring a constant flow of barges between Ky-rock and the shipping terminals. Once shipments reached the terminal they were unloaded by derrick into a steel hopper which was discharged into cars and hauled to a large storage pile.

Chapter 5 **Processing and Shipping**

The pulverized rock asphalt is stored in large piles from which it is loaded by power shovels into flat bottom gondola railroad cars for shipment. During the past year shipments were made to numerous points in 29 states in this country.

This photo was taken from the Kentucky Rock Asphalt Institute Publication on Kentucky Natural Rock Asphalt Specifications and Designs for its many uses in Construction and Maintenance January, 1944.

A large inventory of rock asphalt was maintained at the distribution center usually consisting of hundreds of tons of finished product in a large pile. Rail cars were filled from this large pile for transport to be shipped to destinations as far away as Canada, South America and many states in this country.

Chapter 5 Processing and Shipping

This photo shows rail cars being filled at the Bowling Green Distribution Facility of Kyrock for shipment all over the nation and to surrounding countries.

Chapter 6   Product, Uses and Quality

Since the original geological survey of 1854 numerous studies have documented the rich deposits of "tar sands" or "asphaltic sandstones" in Edmonson County and specifically in the area between Bee Spring and Brownsville, Kentucky.

What made the rock asphalt in this region so special were its unique natural characteristics. Unlike the synthetic hot mix asphalts that are popular today for paving roads Kyrock asphalt possessed characteristics making it superior in several ways. Synthetic "hot mix" asphalt utilizes regular rock or sand aggregate that is not cleaned or purified prior to mixing with the asphalt allowing any impurities to be blended with the mix. Also unlike the hot mix asphalt Kyrock asphalt consisted of a mineral aggregate of pure silica sand granules perfectly coated with natural asphalt. This composition resulted in two unique characteristics. First, the crushed rock asphalt had such a great consistency that it could be re-formed back to its original state with minimal pressure and without any need for heating. Therefore it could be "laid cold" without any special or expensive equipment. It could be delivered to the construction site in regular trucks or trailers and unloaded as needed without worrying about cooling of the mix. Second, it was determined that unlike limestone or other forms of silica bases the silica in Kyrock was so sharp and angular and so hard that it was similar to diamonds in its geological properties that it could cut glass almost as easily as a diamond could. These sharp angular surfaces did not become altered during heavy traffic. This property gave road surfaces high endurance and long lasting anti-skid properties. The surface also remained unreflective while maintaining its original dull black color resulting in better visibility of the road surface.

Since the Kyrock asphalt needed no mixing or heating, it could be stockpiled for future use. Since there were no minute particles in the material to hold moisture it had a long shelf life withstanding years of storage prior to use. After being laid

Chapter 6   Product, Uses and Quality

and rolled, the road surface was ready for traffic. A stockpile could be maintained indefinitely for use in making repairs as needed. Unlike hot-mix asphalt there was very minimal waste since any unused Kyrock material could simply be returned to the storage area or used elsewhere.

There were many uses for rock asphalt from Kyrock. While widely used for paving new roads it found wide acceptance for use on such projects as airport runways, tennis courts, sidewalks, school grounds, recreational areas, railroad station platforms and grade crossings, private estate and cemetery drives, bridge floors and for permanent center line marking on concrete highways and streets. It also was an excellent product for maintenance, repair and resurfacing many old road surfaces such as asphalt, brick, flagstone and concrete. Detailed instructions were provided in Kyrock booklets with engineers at Kentucky Rock Asphalt Company also available to provide any additional information needed to assist the construction company with paving projects.

From the workers to the superintendents everyone at the Kyrock plant was totally dedicated to the quality of the material produced. Mr. Carmichael himself understood and stressed quality at every step of the process. He knew that this was a key factor for assuring the continued success and sales for the company. Without outstanding cleanliness of the rock and adherence to a tight bitumen specification the product would not hold up as a road surface. He implemented procedures throughout the mining and processing stages to ensure consistency and quality of the final product. Even before the rock asphalt was mined at the quarry steps were taken to assure that it was good enough to use at the plant. Future quarry sites were mapped years before being opened and test samples taken from the ledges where rock asphalt was exposed. The samples were taken to nearby cities and

Kentucky
Natural Sandstone Rock Asphalt
●
SPECIFICATIONS AND DESIGNS
for its many uses
in Construction and Maintenance

U. S. 31., Franklin Pike, Nashville, Tenn., surfaced with Kentucky Rock Asphalt in 1929. Frequently referred to as "one of the finest roads in America".

KENTUCKY ROCK ASPHALT INSTITUTE
P. O. Box 32 - - **Louisville, Ky.**
January, 1944

Kentucky Rock Asphalt Company
INCORPORATED
Brownsville, Kentucky

This marketing book was distributed by the company with detailed instructions on Kyrock properties and how to use the product for construction and maintenance.

The views below show the successive stages of repairing a small depression.

Locate depression with a straightedge and mark with a crayon the border of the area to be patched.

Painting depression with liquid asphalt, which is permitted to dry slightly until it is tacky.

Spreading rock asphalt with a rake. The patches are finished by leveling with the lute shown in the "Design of Small Tools," on page 26.

After the rock asphalt is carefully spread it is compacted by tamping or rolling.

Painting an old brick surface with cutback asphalt prior to applying binder. The old brick were held rigid with a cement grout filler.

Feather-edge patch made of Kentucky rock asphalt.

On the Indianapolis Motor Speedway Kentucky rock asphalt was used for patching to correct the roughness of the old brick surface. It produced a more non-skid and hence safer track.

12

This page taken from the Specifications and Designs booklet demonstrates how the Kyrock material could be used to make repairs on surfaces.

Chapter 6   Product, Uses and Quality

WILL NOT CRACK, BREAK OR BUCKLE: Sandstone rock asphalt is sufficiently elastic that it will not crack, break or buckle from its own internal stresses set up by expansion and contraction due to temperature changes. If it is placed upon a solid base that does not crack, there will be no cracks in the surface. If placed upon a rigid type of base such as cement concrete, a sufficient depth of bituminous binder course will reduce the cracking so that it will not be seriously objectionable.

The consistency of Kentucky Rock Asphalt reduces to a minimum any tendency to wrinkle or shove under traffic.

CLEAN AND FREE FROM DUST—REPAIRS OFFER LITTLE INTERFERENCE TO TRAFFIC: This material produces a clean surface, free from dust, that can be used safely at all seasons of the year. It does not require bituminous surface treatments for maintenance, and patches properly made, of the same material under favorable weather conditions, can be used immediately, thus offering the least interference to traffic.

DURABILITY: The surface of sandstone rock asphalt withstands much wear without repair or replacement. It has lasting qualities and is firm enough to withstand the sudden and severe shocks of average traffic. Experience has shown that it produces one of the most durable types of road surfaces when built upon a stable base. This durability is due to several factors, namely: the hardness of the sand grains; the angularity and well-grading of the sand grains which provides a maximum amount of mechanical inter-locking of the aggregate; and the grade of the native asphalt which cements the sand grains.

NON-ABRASIVE: Due to the fact that the sand grains are small and angular, it makes a non-abrasive surface, the aggregate of which does not gouge out parts of the tire with which it comes in contact. The grains of sand produce a maximum effect on a rubber tire insofar as a non-skid surface is concerned, without rupturing the surface of the contact material.

COLOR AND NON-GLARING SURFACE: Sandstone rock asphalt has a dark, dull color and never produces a glare in the driver's eyes. A non-glaring surface will not only aid in preventing accidents, but will also aid in preventing injury to the eyes.

White road surfaces in the bright sunshine are extremely injurious to the eyes. A thin covering of Kentucky rock asphalt spread upon such surfaces will eliminate this glare. The myriads of many-sided silica sand grains in the surface diffuse the light in all directions, thus eliminating the glare.

NON-SKID SURFACE: Sandstone rock asphalt makes the most non-skid type of pavement. This is due to the angularity and hardness of the sand grains. Approximately 95% of the sand in the sandstone rock asphalt from the Kentucky deposits is silica, the compound SiO_2. These sand grains are so hard they will scratch plate glass. Their relative hardness may be judged in comparison with well known materials. The diamond has a hardness of 10.0; silica, 7.0; plate glass, 6.5; iron, 5.0, and the best grade of limestone, 4.0. The extreme hardness of the silica grains causes a sandstone rock asphalt pavement to retain its non-skid features under heavy traffic. The grains do not polish.

Most bank and river sand grains, even though they may be high in silica content, are rounded as a result of erosion. A pavement containing these rounded grains of sand is not so non-skid as a sandstone rock asphalt surface composed of angular grains. Therefore, a theoretical study would indicate that the surface of a pavement consisting of sandstone rock asphalt would be very non-skid. This is proven by actual tests.

The report of Professor R. A. Moyer of Iowa State College, in the December 1933 Proceedings of the Thirteenth Annual meeting of the Highway Research Board, National Research Council, shows a pavement of sandstone rock asphalt to have the highest coefficient of friction with non-skid tread tires of all the standard types of paving materials when the pavement is wet. Additional tests made in 1936 fully confirmed his reports on the 1933 experiments.

The non-skid feature of the road surface is a larger factor each year, as vehicles go at greater speed and with fatalities from auto accidents increasing at a rapid rate. The Engineer designing roads has had a hard time keeping

4

This page from The Kyrock Specifications and Design booklet described the product features.

87

Chapter 6 **Product, Uses and Quality**

Pictures below show some typical applications for asphalt rock from Kyrock. These pages were taken from the Kyrock Specifications and Design booklet.

Playground of Johnson's Wood School, Milwaukee, Wis., surfaced with Kentucky sandstone rock asphalt.

Pennsylvania airport surfaced with Kentucky sandstone rock asphalt.

L. & N. R. R. Station Platform and Driveway surfaced with Kentucky sandstone rock asphalt, Bowling Green, Ky. Its non-skid character makes it safer against accidents.

Kentucky sandstone rock asphalt on concrete bridge floors acts as a shock absorber of traffic impact and protects and waterproofs the concrete structure.

Sidewalk surfaced with Kentucky sandstone rock asphalt, Hot Springs, Virginia.

Driveway in Cave Hill Cemetery, Louisville, Ky., surfaced with Kentucky sandstone rock asphalt. This uniformly dark, non-glaring, noiseless surface is very appropriate for such drives.

6

Chapter 6   Product, Uses and Quality

Main business street, Flemingsburg, Ky. Kentucky Rock Asphalt on 13 per cent grade. Laid 1920.

U. S. Highway 31, Rochester, Indiana—surfaced with Kentucky Rock Asphalt in 1934.

View looking down one of the 150 feet by 4000 feet Kentucky Rock Asphalt Runways. Southern Kentucky Airport.

Kentucky Rock Asphalt on 72nd Street Approach to West Side Highway, New York City.

Private drive in the estate of Mr. Kimberly, Neenah, Wis., surfaced with Kentucky rock asphalt. It is dustless, non-glaring, constant of color. Its pleasing appearance, without cracks, makes a very appropriate surface for a drive on a good-looking estate.

Product, Uses and Quality

The top two photos were taken from the Kyrock Specifications and Design Book showing an old macadam street at Bedford, Ind. before and after surfacing with Kyrock.

This photo shows Madison Pike leading from Covington, KY. To Latonia race track using Kyrock on a concrete base.

Chapter 6   Product, Uses and Quality

A Battery of Tennis Courts in Central Park, New York City. Surfaced with Kentucky Rock Asphalt.

Main Street, Logan, Ohio, ½-inch Kentucky Rock Asphalt wearing surface on bituminous leveling course.

Product, Uses and Quality

spread on sections of existing streets to test its endurance under actual traffic conditions. Sections of a new quarry were measured into fifty foot squares and core drilled to determine the depth and thickness of the rock asphalt layer. Every twelve inches of the core samples were carefully analyzed by the laboratory to determine the bitumen content. Based on this testing the quarry operators knew exactly how much overburden to remove to reach the desired rock asphalt layer. Great care was then taken at the quarry to remove and clean any dirt or debris from the rock. After thoroughly cleaning the layer of rock asphalt, it was "shot" with dynamite to break it up into small enough pieces for loading. At this point more samples were taken for bitumen testing at the laboratory. If the test results were acceptable then asphalt rocks were hand-picked by workmen who were experts in selecting material with the correct bitumen content. No steam shovels were used to load this rock since they might add some dirt or other contaminants to the material. It was either loaded by hand or by derrick depending on size.

Asphalt rock coming in from the various quarries went through several stages of mixing to assure uniformity of finished product. After passing through the main crusher a conveyor belt carried the material to an area called the "bullpen" where a series of trip gate bins of one-ton capacity each contained rock asphalt with differing bitumen content. These bins could be open or closed to release rock onto the conveyor to obtain material containing the optimum bitumen content prior to further crushing. After passing through a secondary crusher a series of rollers and screens provided additional mixing that gave additional uniformity. At each stage of the plant process the rock asphalt was under strict laboratory control. Even during the barge loading additional mixing of the final granular material was done by keeping the barge in constant motion. In addition, at the distribution facility

Chapter 6   Product, Uses and Quality

2.0 MATERIALS.

    2.1 Rock Asphalt: This rock asphalt shall be composed of sharp, angular quartz sand, impregnated by natural processes with bitumen native to the rock. The sand in the rock asphalt shall contain not less than 93.0% silica (SiO_2). It shall be free from dirt, vegetable or other foreign material.

    2.2 Gradation: The rock asphalt shall be so crushed and ground that it will meet the following requirements by weight when tested by laboratory methods using square mesh sieves:

PROPORTIONATE AMOUNT	Per Cent
Retained on ¾ inch sieve	0
Retained on ½ inch sieve not more than	1
Retained on No. 4 sieve not more than	20

    2.3 Bitumen Content: The ignition method will be considered as the standard laboratory test to determine the bitumen content. The loss on ignition shall be not less than 7.2% nor more than 9.0%. The loss by extraction method shall be not less than 6.3% nor more than 8.5%.

    2.4 Source of Supply: The rock asphalt for this item shall be a sandstone rock asphalt obtained from a source from which for a period of at least two (2) consecutive years immediately prior to taking bids has been produced sandstone rock asphalt laid in pavements giving satisfactory service when used as a natural non-treated paving material. The rock asphalt shall be prepared at a plant capable of maintaining the required uniformity of quality at the necessary rate of production. Approval of source of supply of the sandrock asphalt furnished under these specifications shall be obtained from the engineer prior to delivery of material. Samples shall be submitted as directed.

This section from the Kyrock Specification and Designs Booklet specifies the requirement for rock asphalt produced at the Kyrock Plant. Note the tight specification for silica, granular size and Bitumen Content. The material had to also meet a use test whereby the material had been evaluated as a pavement material at least two years prior to taking bids for using the material.

another mixing occurred when the latest month's production was mixed with the previous one.

The plant used a tighter self-imposed internal specification than the published one. Nothing was shipped outside 6 to 8% bitumen content with most shipments averaging 7.1% varying by no more than 0.3%. Low bitumen content or excessive dirt in the Kyrock finished material could lead to cracks causing the pavement to break up prematurely shortening the lifetime of the road. If the bitumen content was too high the pavement would have a tarry surface that melted in hot weather or formed ruts or wash boards and also reduced the lifetime of the road.

Chapter 6   Product, Uses and Quality

Laboratory

Lon Johnson, Walter Sally, Wells Hackney, one man is unidentified.

This is a photograph of the main Kyrock Laboratory where quarry samples and finished rock asphalt production samples were continuously being tested. Approximately every 100 pounds of finished product was tested to assure quality and uniformity.

94

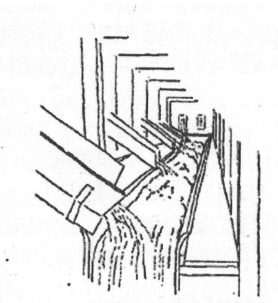

Another thorough mixing follows the second and third disintegrating processes. Again the material is separated to feed simultaneously through six pulverizing mills and recollected in volume as illustrated.

Finished Kyrock is delivered into 400-ton barges. Again thoroughly mixed by keeping barge in motion under delivery spout.

These drawings taken from the Kyrock publication "The Story of Kyrock" describe some of the several methods used to assure mixing and uniformity of the finished product.

Chapter 6   Product, Uses and Quality

The Kyrock laboratory at the distribution point in Bowling Green, KY made final checks on the quality of the shipments from that facility to assure proper bitumen content and mixing.

There may be some who think that the quality control measures taken by Kyrock were a bit excessive, but these measures were proven to assure a final product that demonstrated outstanding quality and endurance.   The later easing of these controls may have been a contributing factor in the eventual closing of Kyrock.

Chapter 7　Workers, Jobs and Safety

Due to the somewhat rugged and isolated nature of the area around Kyrock there were essentially few jobs available at the time the Kyrock plant started its operations. Most of the accessible timber had been cleared and inhabitants of the area depended primarily on farming to make a living. A highly skilled work force was needed to operate the many large pieces of equipment and to perform the jobs necessary to produce top quality rock asphalt. It was left to Mr. Carmichael and the few people he assembled around him to hire and train a suitable work force. Quarry workers who knew how to find and mine the rock asphalt deposits needed skills to operate steam powered shovels, derricks, locomotives, air drills and other pieces of equipment. Knowledge and training with dynamite used at the quarry was essential. Others needed skills in operating and maintaining the processing equipment consisting of conveyors, crushers and milling/grinding machines. Track Crews ("Gangs") were needed for building, moving and maintaining railroad tracks. Carpenters were needed to construct the many buildings around the plant as well as houses for workers. People were needed for all these jobs and more.

Mr. Carmichael relied on his knowledge and vast experience to get the workforce trained. He actively recruited people from the engineering and coal mining fields to come and work at Kyrock. Since few of the workers had experience in any of these jobs, "on the job training" had to be used in most cases. There was no formal job training procedure. Many workers started out at low skilled positions and worked their way up to the better paid more highly skilled jobs by just watching and learning how to operate equipment. Most of the employees at Kyrock were local people while some of the higher skilled and supervisory jobs were filled with people from out of state. About 500 people were employed by the company but other jobs were likely created by just its presence in the area.

This photo shows the Office Force at Kyrock. From the right side of the photo (corner post) are Pete Wilson-Assistant Office Manager, Wells Hackney, Albert Porter-Night Watch-man/Locomotives, Paul Miller, H. St. G. T. Carmichael-Plant Superintendent, Unidentified Man and Woman, Robert Clement, Lee Percy-Office Manager, Clarence Harrison-Deliveryman (in wagon). Here at the office business operation, clerical matters as well as time keeping for worker's pay were handled. Signs above windows to left are believed to read "Time Keeper" and "Supply Clerk". On the right a sign states "Get Money Orders Here".

Chapter 7 **Workers, Jobs and Safety**

*April 1. Office, Commissary and other employees taken on Kyrock Office Steps.
January flood put water two feet over windows shown. Top to bottom, left to right:
Chester Luttrell, unidentified, Jewell "Tillie" Hinton, Bill Garvin, Wells Hackney,
Hooper Knight, Walter Salley, Lee Percy, Wand B. Doyell.*

This photo was likely taken after the Jan. 1937 flood.

Probably some of the most desirable jobs were those at the commissary or office.
Most of these went to the more educated or skilled workers in the area or in some
cases to those recruited by Mr. Carmichael from outside the Kyrock community.
Extracting and processing asphalt rock required hard, dirty and sometimes dangerous work with long hours and few breaks. Not only did the hillside have to

Chapter 7   Workers, Jobs and Safety

This photo shows a group of Kyrock workers at Quarry No. 1 breaking up, sorting and loading rock asphalt rock while a nearby derrick loads the large rock boulders. Track crews ("gangs") laid the tracks so that Dinkey operators could pull them to the crushing plant.

be stripped of the top layer of soil referred to as overburden but the rock below had to be broken up using explosives. Using dynamite could be tricky and dangerous if something went wrong during the process of exploding the rock into pieces small enough to be further broken down for transport and processing. Nothing over about 4 feet in diameter could be loaded into the dinkeys for transport to the crusher. Larger pieces had to be broken down by hand or further exploded. Using picks

Chapter 7   Workers, Jobs and Safety

Rumsey Harrison and Morris Webb working with cored driller ca. 1922-1924.

Walter Webb and Rumsey Harrison with core drill ca. 1922-1924.

One of the jobs at Kyrock was Core Driller where samples were taken below the overburden layer to check the depth and quality of the asphalt rock layer. Holes also had to be drilled for dynamite to be inserted for blasting the overburden layer or to break up the rock asphalt.

Chapter 7   Workers, Jobs and Safety

In this photo workers at the processing plant can be seen covered with dust and dirt while working on equipment.

or hammers to break up rock was hard work that could result in injuries if not careful. The smaller pieces of rock had to be loaded by hand into boxes but required heavy lifting. Workers had to watch for falling rocks and extreme caution was needed working around large steam shovels, derricks and dinkeys. Processing the rock further into the desired particle size involved using a large crusher and hammer mill. Work at the processing plant could be dirty and dusty and could lead

Chapter 7   Workers, Jobs and Safety

Young workers pose for a photo nearby dinkeys at the quarry. They were probably too young to operate the dinkeys.

to health problems later in life. The possibility of being injured during these operations was high even with extreme caution.

The dinkeys used to pull loads of rock or asphalt could be dangerous in many ways. To prevent collisions switchmen used telephones along the tracks to make sure they knew the exact location of every dinkey. Unbalanced loads of rock could cause the cars to jump track spilling the load or being derailed. Rocks might drop off the train ahead and knock some of the cars off the track or the engine could "drop some fire" setting a tie ablaze. Track crews were always nearby to take care of these problems but there was always potential for accidents.

Chapter 7   Workers, Jobs and Safety

No 23 Dinkey Engine at Kyrock. Shelby Ashley is standing beside engine which he operated. Engineers, Brakemen, Switchmen, Mechanics and Track Crews were needed to keep Dinkeys in operation. Accidents involving Dinkeys were a fairly common occurrence.

Workers did not wear safety equipment such as safety shoes, safety glasses or hard hats at the quarries, processing plant and machine shops.   None of the Laboratory workers wore safety glasses or other safety apparel while working with chemicals or equipment, although those jobs were probably some of the safest jobs in the plant.

Chapter 7 Workers, Jobs and Safety

There are no known documented records for accidents at Kyrock. Until 1970 when the Occupational Safety and Health Administration (OSHA) and in 1978 when the Mine Safety and Health Administration (MSHA) were established accident investigation and prevention was left primarily up to a company. At Kyrock the only accounts of accidents have been described by former workers at Kyrock. No doubt there were numerous untold accidents and many "minor" injuries that were never mentioned. All accidents were thoroughly investigated and being as concerned a humanitarian as Mr. Carmichael was I am sure he did his best to prevent these accidents but there was not the emphasis on safety that companies today are required to take. In all fairness the industry standard for safety was very low at the time and most companies were not required to comply with standards like we have today. Workers assumed that the hazards involved in the work were just a part of the job and were willing to take on the risk of injury to earn an acceptable wage.

Some of the accidents that happened at Kyrock have been described by former workers. Many of these were from interviews recorded from workers for the Oral History Project done in 1981 by Western Kentucky University students. These are listed below but should be considered as unofficial reports.

Former Kyrock employee Roy Hazlip described how a dinkey he was driving pulling a whole string of cars ran off the track over the dump and he barely escaped injury by jumping off the dinkey.

Former Kyrock employee Percy Davis described two dinkey accidents where men were killed. On one incident a dinkey operator was run over by his dinkey when it went out of control and ran over a hillside running over the man's legs, cutting off both of them. He later died at the hospital.

Chapter 7   Workers, Jobs and Safety

Although one of the safer jobs Laboratory workers were not required to wear any safety apparel.

Mr. Davis described another incident where a boy was run over by a dinkey causing serious internal injuries and he later died at the hospital.

Another former Kyrock worker, Anderson Lashley, described an accident in which a wagon carrying two women was struck by a dinkey when the wagon got stuck on the railroad tracks. The wagon's "rough lock", a chain wrapped around the rear wheel, had become lodged around the ball of the rail and the wagon could not go forward or backward. Despite the desperate screams from the man who had gotten

This early photo of a machine shop at Kyrock shows workers dressed for hard work but with no safety equipment like safety goggles around pieces of flying metal.

off the wagon to try to get the dinkey operator to stop, it could not be stopped in time. The dinkey which was pulling 19 cars of rock asphalt ran over the wagon killing both women. Apparently there were many accidents involving dinkeys many involving other than Kyrock employees. Former Kyrock employee Owen Prunty stated that the sons of fellow Kyrock employees Lacy Minton and Bill Stewart were also killed by dinkeys.

An accident reported by former Kyrock employees Anderson Lashley and Blaine Vincent involved an explosion at the cap house where caps were being placed on dynamite sticks. Instead of using a wooden peg to insert the cap onto the dynamite stick the worker mistakenly used a metal peg that was not permitted by the procedure for the job. The dynamite exploded killing two of the three workers and left the third man with a burst ear drum, blindness in one eye and about 100 pieces of copper wire in his right side.

Former Kyrock employees Walter Davis, Walter Gipson and Roy Hazlip described an accident that occurred while clearing space for a rail line to the Morris Quarry. One of the workers setting off dynamite to clear the trail got behind a tree to protect him from the blast but a rock from the blast came down hitting him on the head causing fatal injuries.

Mr. Gipson also described the following accidents.   A man was picking up rocks to load into wagons when another large rock weighing perhaps fifteen tons became dislodged and rolled over him killing him. Another fatal accident occurred when workers were cleaning out the large crusher which had to be cleaned occasionally to remove the sticky asphalt that collected on it. The large lid weighing 1500 pounds had to be raised by four or five men to gain access to the inside of the crusher. After the worker Jack Woodcock had finished cleaning the inside of the crusher he screamed out "let her down" to let the other workers know that the lid could be closed. He made the fatal mistake of moving his head too close to the area where the lid came down and killed him instantly.

The accidents reported here are probably but a few of those that happened at Kyrock but are likely the most serious ones that employees remembered. These accidents are probably typical for the type of work performed at Kyrock.

Chapter 8 **Commissary at Kyrock**

Entrance To Kyrock Plant

This is the bridge over Sweet Spring leading from the commissary to the Kyrock Plant. It appears to have been recently built when this photo was taken in the 1920's or 30's. The bridge was apparently mainly used for pedestrians walking to the plant. The swinging bridge (out of sight) leading to the crusher was located just to the left at the end of this bridge. The sign to the left of the bridge warns people "You must not use Sweet Spring water to wash cars". There appears to be a bulletin board under the Kyrock sign for employee postings.

At the top of the photo is a barn for the horses kept at the plant. On the right side of the bridge is one of the houses built by the company, probably used by the person attending the horses.

109

Chapter 8   Commissary at Kyrock

At one time as many as 1500 workers were estimated to be on payroll at Kyrock but typically about 500 or more worked there all of whom needed food, supplies and other necessities for them and their families. At that time most people could not afford to buy an automobile to travel to the larger towns for these things. Most of the workers had little money to spend especially during winter months when work at the company was slowed or suspended by bad weather. Having worked in the coal fields and at the Old Hickory Powder Plant in Oak Ridge Mr. Carmichael was experienced in the needs of mining and company communities. With company support and the help of capable employees he built commissaries where basic food and other necessities could be purchased. The main commissary was built near the canal at Nolin Landing close to the community of Bluetown. Smaller commissaries were established nearby Sweeden, Indian Creek and Black Gold. These were like branch locations that were kept stocked by the main commissary at Kyrock allowing most area residents to travel only a few miles to reach. Convenient store hours were scheduled to open at 6:00 AM and remain open until 8:00 PM, allowing people to stop by after work to order or pick up supplies.

Former employees at the commissaries believed that thousands of people shopped there. To keep them stocked with the correct items and inventory levels clerks would order supplies either by mail or telephone. They also handled requisitions from the plant for parts and supplies to keep it running. All these groceries and supplies were shipped from Bowling Green, Kentucky by steamboat and barge. There were limits to the kinds of items carried by the commissaries. No fancy items like men's suits or women's ready-made dresses were available. There was not enough space to stock hardware. Basic everyday necessities like groceries,

110

Chapter 8 **Commissary at Kyrock**

Kentucky Rock Asphalt Co. Commissary

This is believed to be a photo of the original commissary built at Kyrock in the early 1920's. Walter Davis, who worked at the commissary between 1919 and 1930, described how an outdoor movie theater was built next to the commissary during that time. This can be seen on the upper side of the commissary. On the left side is located the dentist office and on the right side next to the outdoor movie theater are houses built for Kyrock employees. The original commissary burned in the 1930's and was rebuilt in the same location.

work clothes, shoes, hats, ladies blouses, hose and piece good material to make clothes were sold. Beef was shipped from a Bowling Green packing house, while pork was obtained from local farmers. They were kept in a freezer adjacent to the

Chapter 8   Commissary at Kyrock

This is a clip taken from a bird's eye view of Kyrock which shows the first Commissary from another angle. The outdoor movie theater and dentist office can be seen on each side of the commissary.

main commissary. Ice was available for those who were fortunate enough to own ice boxes. In the beginning the ice had to be shipped in by boat from Bowling Green resulting in a 10 to 15% loss due to melting before it even reached the commissary. Later on the company built an ice plant near the commissary where

Chapter 8   **Commissary at Kyrock**

This photo shows another view of the commissary after the outside movie theater was moved to the school building and the Office was built in its place. Some of the buildings in the picture are Hospital/Clinic (left), Commissary, Office Building, Administrative Supply Office and workers' houses. The picture was taken by Borst Photo around the early 1920's.

they made their own ice and sold for 50 to 75 cents per 100 pounds. Kerosene cost about 10 to 15 cents per gallon and along with ice could be delivered by wagon. The commissaries were intended to be non-profit and competitive with nearby groceries that were scattered throughout the area. It was still difficult for some people to make ends meet even working long hours. Various systems of credit

Chapter 8   Commissary at Kyrock

This is a photo of the Kyrock Commissary year unknown, possibly rebuilt after the original commissary burned.

were developed to help them extend bills to a later time when wages could be used to pay them. At first the company tried to issue scrip often called "script" as a means of credit. It resembled a large brass penny and had values of a nickel, dime, quarter, fifty cents and dollar. Workers who requested scrip issued to them would go to the payroll window where their name, work number and value of the scrip

Chapter 8 **Commissary at Kyrock**

Kentucky Rock Asphalt Co. Inc., Commissary No. 2 located at Sweeden, KY. A group of high school students on their way to be tested for an academic team. From left: Hubert Brooks, Coy Parsley, Elbert Meredith, Hoyt Parsley, Earl Reed, Clorene Harrison Lane, Arnold A. Van Meter.

This is a photo of Commissary No. 2 located at Sweeden, Kentucky. It was a branch of the main commissary at Kyrock which kept this one and other branches located at Indian Creek and Black Gold stocked with basic supplies.

given to them was recorded. When pay day arrived either on the fifteenth or last day of the month, the value of the scrip issued to them was deducted from their pay. The practice of issuing scrip as a means of credit was later abandoned because workers would sometimes lose or misplace the coins and come back to the commissary complaining that they could not keep track of it. The company then tried using another form of credit known as "scrip cards" which were issued to workers for certain amounts and deducted from their pay at the next pay period.

Chapter 8   Commissary at Kyrock

Each time the person purchased something at the commissary on credit that amount was punched out on the card until the value on the card was depleted, very similar to gift cards currently used at some stores today. Sometimes children

Scrip similar to the piece pictured below was issued to workers as a form of credit when Kyrock began opera-tions in the early 1920's. Use of these coins was discontinued after about a year and replaced with punch cards that were also abandoned and re-placed with a credit system where bills were deducted from pay at each payday cycle.

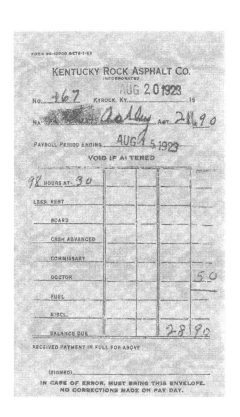

would find depleted cards with a penny or so remaining on them and take them back to the commissary to get candy with any value left on the card. After about a year of using the "scrip cards" they were also abandoned in favor of just a simple line of credit where the amount owed to the commissary was merely deducted from the worker's pay. The busiest days for the commissary were always the first and

Chapter 8   Commissary at Kyrock

sixteenth day of each month-one day after each payday. That was because the workers would have two full weeks before their bill was deducted from their pay. Orders were taken by the commissary clerks and organized by communities at Kyrock, Woodside, Ridgedale and outlying areas that were accessible within a few miles. Since most of the customers did not have a means of getting the orders to their homes the commissary provided a delivery service to each community. For many years the delivery man named Clarence Harrison with his beautiful large, gray Persian mare fittingly named "Beauty" pulled a heavily loaded wagon and trailer for several miles to each of these areas delivering customers' orders. The wagon had a large bed with a removable seat where a small tank of kerosene was located underneath. Mr. Harrison would work in the commissary until the company whistle blew at 6:00 AM and then would load up the wagon and trailer to begin making the deliveries by 6:30 AM. The trips over rough, hilly roads carrying everything from groceries to kerosene and ice could be very difficult at times, especially during winter. Mr. Harrison recalled once how his wagon single tree used for hooking the wagon to his horse broke causing him to lose an entire load of ice. Once a young boy fell off his delivery wagon and on another occasion a large chunk of ice fell striking a woman on her head finally landing on his foot thankfully without any serious injuries. He stated that "On script day they run me to death" and "...I worked like a mule down there". He made the best of the situation becoming very fond of his horse Beauty who he spoiled by giving her sugar or candy. The customers who lived in areas where their goods could not be delivered by the commissary had to get their things home by any means possible. My mother, who lived in an area of Edmonson County known as the "forks" relayed a story to me of

Chapter 8 **Commissary at Kyrock**

This is a photo of Clarence Harrison who delivered groceries and other goods from the Commissary to nearby communities around the Kyrock Plant.

when she was only seven years old and her mother made a trip from the river bottom farm they worked to get some groceries at the Kyrock commissary. My grandmother crossed the river in their "Jo" boat, but when she returned someone had used the boat to get back to the other side of the river. After calling for my mother who was watching over her younger siblings she was able to give her instructions on how to row the boat back to the Kyrock side so that my grandmother could cross back over the river.

Some of the many responsibilities of the Kyrock commissary were keeping track of workers' time sheets, pay rate, charges at the commissary and making sure the

Chapter 8 **Commissary at Kyrock**

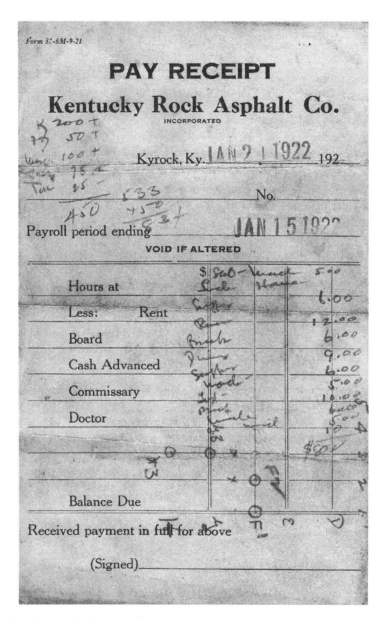

This is a sample of a discarded payroll receipt that was filled out by the payroll clerk showing deductions made from a worker's pay for period ending Jan 15, 1922.

correct pay was given to each worker. Former commissary clerk and timekeeper Walter Davis recalled how many times he would work long hours sometimes until midnight or 1 A.M. They would close time sheets on the 15th and last day of the month and pass out money on the 20th and 5th of each month to 500 workers or

Chapter 8   Commissary at Kyrock

more.   Only cash was distributed meaning that a typical payroll ranged from $15,000 to $18,000. This amount had to be transported from the Brownsville Deposit Bank to the Kyrock commissary twice a month to meet payroll requirements. When the dirt road from Brownsville was passable by automobile the company would send three cars to transport the money. The car containing the money was guarded by armed men in the other two cars one in front and one in the rear. During times when the road from Brownsville was not passable by automobile especially during winter the payroll had to be brought in by horseback. Seven heavily armed men each on horseback were used with three in the front and three in the back with the middle horse carrying the payroll money safely stuffed away in its saddle bags. Occasionally the company yacht, no doubt heavily armed, would be used to transport the money down the river to Kyrock. Fortunately, no attempt was ever reported of an attempted robbery of the payroll during transit from Brownsville. There was, however, a break-in of the company safe located in the commissary and the cash was never recovered.

The commissary work force grew over the years as business increased and the staff assumed more responsibilities. Eventually the main commissary had eight to ten employees with another two or three at each of the branch commissaries. The commissaries as well as the local stores around Kyrock were an important part of the area, providing groceries and supplies to the residents that they would otherwise have been unable to obtain. Today these have been replaced with convenience stores or large grocery chains where the personal service and a friendly family atmosphere of these once busy establishments are surely missed.

Chapter 9   Communities and Housing

Prior to the opening of Kyrock most inhabitants of Edmonson County Kentucky derived a meager living primarily from farming and logging among the beautiful hills and valleys of the area. The population was sparse with only a few houses close to the Kyrock plant. Much of the land around the plant was owned by the company. Realizing that housing was needed for the workers, the company built houses and two hotels to accommodate the large workforce needed to run the plant. The individual groups of company built houses were referred to as "communities" or "camps", but are probably best described as neighborhoods.

This is a birds-eye view of some of the first houses built by Kyrock. The bottom row of houses is believed to be on River Road and the upper row at Bluetown.

Chapter 9 Communities and Housing

The most well-known of the Kyrock communities were Woodside, Ridgedale and Bluetown, although two other smaller ones were located on River Road and Sweet Spring Road. The houses near the plant were at Bluetown, River Road and Sweet Spring Road. These houses were probably less desirable due to the proximity to hills and the flood plain.

To get to the communities from Brownsville you traveled on former Highway 65 (now Highway 259) until turning right onto the old Kyrock Road at Sweeden, Kentucky. When traveling on this road it took a turn to the right where one of the company hotels called the Log Hotel was located on the left. Here also was located Dr. Cornwell's house and office, the former company doctor. At this point

This is a photo of the original Log Hotel built at Woodside in 1918. It was used to house visitors and single workers who did not have a home near Kyrock.

Chapter 9 **Communities and Housing**

Log house Ky. Rock Asphalt Co.

Borst Photo

This is a later photo of the Log Hotel which at one time was used for Kindergarten students.

the road sloped downward and took a sharp turn to the left where it was paved with substandard asphalt. Here Lane's Store, a privately owned store operated by Ernest and Clorene Lane, was located. Traveling a bit farther you came to the first Kyrock community called Woodside where 20 to 30 houses were present. The houses were on both sides of the road only a few yards apart with very similar size and style. Continuing down the road led to another privately owned store operated by Claude Saling. Woodside community extended little more than about a quarter mile from Lane's Store.

Chapter 9 **Communities and Housing**

This photo shows the houses at Woodside Community as they appeared in the 1920's.

Leaving Woodside the road made a curve to the right and entered the community of Ridgedale where another group of 20 to 30 houses similar to those at Woodside were located. *Kyrock Kentucky* states that "along the main road through Ridgedale Camp is where many of the first and oldest company houses were found. Many families lived in each house as the families grew with children or got smaller as members left to do other work or to marry." As you traveled further down the road through Ridgedale you could see Kyrock Church on the left side of the road on a steep hill. The church posed as a highly visible landmark on the hilltop with its

Chapter 9   **Communities and Housing**

This is the Ridgedale Community as seen from the hillside near Woodside Community.

Ridgedale houses were located just below the hill where Kyrock Church was built.

Chapter 9 Communities and Housing

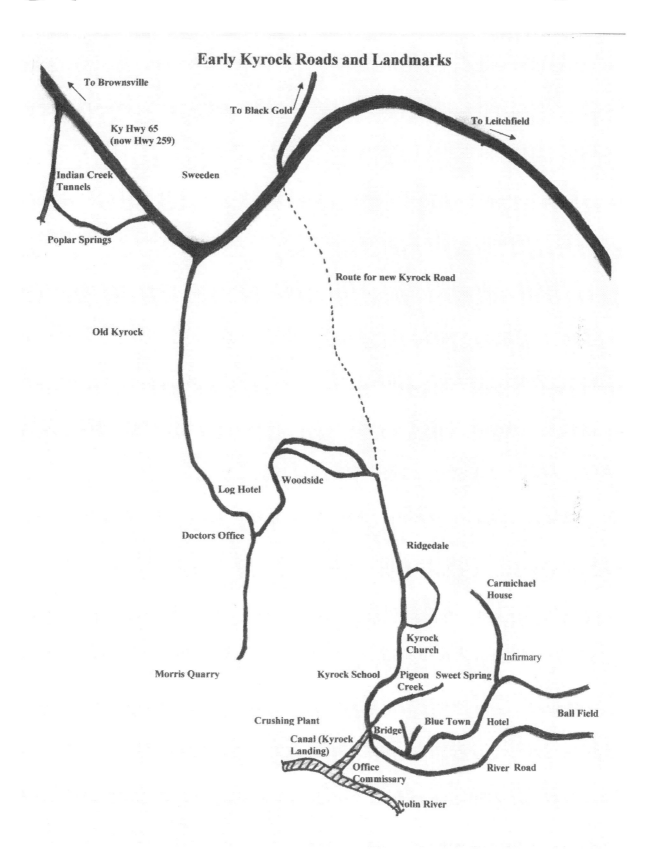

Early Kyrock Roads and Landmarks

To Brownsville

Ky Hwy 65
(now Hwy 259)

To Black Gold

To Leitchfield

Indian Creek
Tunnels

Sweeden

Poplar Springs

Route for new Kyrock Road

Old Kyrock

Log Hotel

Woodside

Doctors Office

Ridgedale

Carmichael
House

Infirmary

Morris Quarry

Kyrock School

Kyrock
Church

Pigeon
Creek

Sweet Spring

Crushing Plant

Bridge

Blue Town

Hotel

Ball Field

Canal (Kyrock
Landing)

Office
Commissary

River Road

Nolin River

Chapter 9   **Communities and Housing**

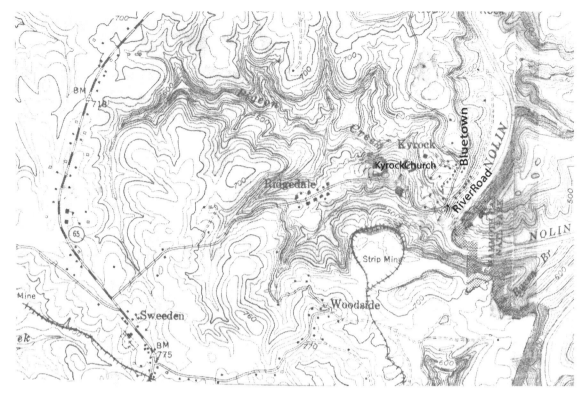

This map shows the location of Woodside and Ridgedale Communities. River Row camps are shown nearby the Nolin River with Bluetown located on the hillside above.

white lap siding and large bronze bell mounted in the steeple. Continuing down the road at the bottom of the hill was the bridge over Sweet Spring, Pigeon Hollow on the left with the canal to the right where asphalt was loaded onto the barges for shipment. Here you could begin to see indications of the plant operations where buildings that housed the office, commissary and post office were located. Continuing on up the road to the river bottoms you would see a group of houses referred to by most as "River Road Camp" or "River Row". This community consisted of about ten houses built high on "stilts" to protect them from flooding by nearby Nolin River. At the end of the road you could look across the river and see another area landmark called dismal rock. Older residents of this area recalled

Chapter 9   Communities and Housing

This aerial view shows Ridgedale Community with Woodside Community on the hillside above. On the hillside just up from Ridgedale the Kyrock Church can be seen. Near the river are River Road and Bluetown Communities.

that the crack in this rock has gotten significantly wider since their childhood when Kyrock first opened. In this area was also located Wagon Shed Rock and Turkey Foot Cave. Nearby here was where some of the Kyrock workers who lived in what was referred to as the "forks of the river" would cross Nolin River after walking miles from their homes to reach work. The "forks of the river" described the section of Edmonson County between the forks of Nolin and Green Rivers.

Chapter 9 Communities and Housing

This photo of Dismal Rock, known for being a landmark near Kyrock shows how it would have looked from Kyrock with the distinctive crack which is said to have gotten wider over the years.

Returning from River Road to the bridge near Sweet Spring you could turn right toward Pigeon Hollow on a paved section of road called Asphalt Hill. A trip up this steep incline led to the community of Bluetown where about 20 more company

Chapter 9 Communities and Housing

owned houses were located. Today no one knows for sure why the community was called Bluetown, since the houses were all painted the standard company green color. Houses here were scattered along both sides of the road and the other hotel called Bluetown Hotel was on the top of the hill on the right side of the road overlooking River Road and the Nolin River.

Some of the houses at Kyrock were built high off the ground to protect them from flooding in flood-prone areas such as those on River Road.

At its peak about 2000 people lived in and around the Kyrock communities making this their home for many years depending on the Kyrock plant for their income and in many cases their housing. The houses built by Kyrock were mostly small boxed houses constructed very similar to the way a barn would be built today. A staff of

Chapter 9 **Communities and Housing**

This is a photo of the Bluetown Hotel-one of the first structures built at Kyrock. Notice the porch was built to include an existing tree.

Kyrock carpenters built and maintained the houses. Most were L-shaped or rectangular with three to four rooms consisting of a living room, kitchen, and one or two bedrooms. The main section of the house had gabled ends consisting of a living room and one bedroom sometimes with a front porch across the front. The porch had a flat top with white posts supporting it. The kitchen was in the rear section of the house and also had a flat or slightly sloped roof. If there was an extra bedroom, it was in this section. It was not unusual to see some homes with beds in the living room and kitchen if there was a large family living in the house.

Chapter 9 **Communities and Housing**

The houses sat on wood posts or stone pillars and each had a brick chimney or possibly two that serviced the heating stove in the living room and the cook stove in the kitchen. There was typically an outhouse and sometimes a small storage building in the back yard. The houses were covered with vertical pine planks on the outside with the opposite sides of these planks serving as the inside walls. Narrow wood strips were placed over the vertical cracks between the planks on the outside of the house. Planks were also used to make the floors and ceilings, but without wood strips to cover the cracks. The outside of the houses were painted green and black tar paper was used to cover the roofs. The buildings had an open foundation that was sometimes covered with lattice. Some of the former inhabitants remembered how neighborhood children would sometimes spend their free time playing under the houses.

Most occupants of the Kyrock houses probably considered themselves fortunate to be able to live in such a nice house as those provided to them. The houses were neat, clean and appeared well built. The rent was low and the houses were maintained by the company. There was water in or nearby their home and a store or commissary was available to purchase food and supplies. But living conditions compared to today's standards were still difficult. Occupants of the houses usually used newspapers to cover inside walls to block the cold air during winter. Use of insulation in the walls was unheard of at the time and probably would have been almost impossible to install on the plank walls. In winter the houses were cold and drafty, heated only with a wood or coal stove located in the living room. The pine plank floors had cracks wide enough to see the ground below, sometimes seeing chickens or animals milling around underneath them. The houses were only modestly decorated with very few having even rugs on the floors. One former

Chapter 9 Communities and Housing

inhabitant described using white sand to sprinkle on the floor to help clean off the dirt and debris. There was no inside plumbing with water piped from Sweet Spring or taken from wells. Outhouses were used for toilets. In the summer windows and doors without screens were opened to capture a cool breeze. Electricity was not available for houses until about the 1940's, so that the only source for light was usually a coal oil lamp. Some families did benefit from the luxury of an ice box, ice being available from the local commissary. Still, most former inhabitants of the Kyrock Communities had only fond memories of their experiences there. There was a sincere feeling of belonging to a tight knit neighborhood where people cared for and helped their neighbors when needed.

This was a typical house built in the Woodside Community near the "old crooked tree".

Chapter 9 **Communities and Housing**

Many of the approximately 500 employees of Kyrock did not live in company built houses. Some lived in either the company hotels or in outlying areas. The hotel located at Woodside near the doctor's office was called the "Log Hotel". It was a two story eight room rectangular log building with gabled ends. Lesser important visitors or workers far from home stayed at this hotel. Out of state workers like those who came from Alabama to build the canal probably stayed there. At one time several families lived in this building. It was later used as a hospital and also as a kindergarten. The Blue Hotel in Bluetown Community was used for the more important guests like company officials or dignitaries who occasionally made visits to Kyrock. Bluetown Hotel was a frame rectangular building with a two story section on the left side and a single story that had a front porch. It had a gabled roof and contained about ten rooms. One distinguishing feature was the tree that was left growing through the front porch. The Kyrock workers who lived in outlying areas made daily trips from their homes in nearby rural areas. Some from my own family walked up the hills and through the hollows to cross nearby Nolin River to the plant. The daily trip was at times probably extremely tiring to a person who had already worked long and hard at the plant or in the quarry. Still, there were few complaints from workers who were just thankful to have a job that allowed them the opportunity to work near their home and provide income to support their families.

Chapter 10 **Kyrock Church and School**

In the 1920's small community schools were sprinkled throughout Edmonson County Kentucky in fairly remote locations. Most inhabitants did not own automobiles or other modes of transportation for their children to travel more than a few miles to school. Elementary schools like Sweeden, Cove Hollow, Ollie, Union Light, Poplar Springs and others were established to provide opportunities for children living far away from the larger communities with schools that were usually closer to their homes. These small one room schools not only provided a building for the school, but could also be used for church services.

With the exception of a small group of Catholics in the Sunfish community of the county nearly all the inhabitants were Baptists. When the Kyrock operation was established and Mr. Carmichael became superintendent he realized that a community school and church would be needed for the many workers pouring into the Kyrock community. He immediately took on the task of establishing a church close to the Kyrock facility that the workers could attend. It would be separate from the school and suitable for all the community to attend. He realized that his Episcopalian religion would not fit into a community dominated by Baptists. He decided on a compromise and instead decided to make the new church part of the Methodist affiliation, no doubt thinking it was probably close enough to the Baptist belief that there would be no problems with all the nearby inhabitants attending. He also had connections with people in the cities of Louisville and Bowling Green that probably made it easier to establish the church as Methodist. Whatever his intent, there seemed to be little controversy generated in the Kyrock community.

In 1924 Kyrock Methodist Church was established consisting of only thirteen members headed by pastor H.C. (Homer) Ogles. Mr. Carmichael arranged for land to be donated by the company where a church could be built. Reverend Ogles

Chapter 10 **Kyrock Church and School**

recommended the church be built on "the big rock at the east end of the little village Ridgedale" and Mr. Carmichael gave his approval for the site. The company furnished materials and labor for construction of the building. Monetary donations from some of the workers were also used to help buy materials and supplies. A deed was issued on July 13, 1925 for "a certain lot or parcel of land situated on the top of the round knob or hill at the east end of Ridgedale Village in Kyrock Camp containing 100 feet by 150 feet with the church house recently constructed being located in the center thereof, with right of way to and from said church to the Kyrock and Sweeden public road". The large frame building constructed was covered with weather boarding painted white and a black rubberized roofing. Approximately 55 steps had to be built to reach to the top of the hill and to the front door. A large bronze bell donated to the Sunday school by supporters from New York City was mounted in the rear of the building. The inside walls of the church were covered with tongue and groove lumber and two rows of pews were arranged for seating. The building was lighted by electricity which was supplied by a dynamo located at the Kyrock plant.

The church made an impressive view from the small village of Ridgedale just below the hill. The steep climb up the steps on the large rock up to the double front doors of the large frame building with a large cupola on the roof near the front door must have been a sight to behold. It had been constructed on concrete supports resting on the solid rock. Storms would take their toll on the building since it had no cushioning from dirt below the concrete supports. Pews would sometimes have to be placed against the front doors or held shut by men during storms. One could only imagine how the building must have shook and vibrated during some of

Chapter 10   Kyrock Church and School

Kyrock Church was built on a large rock above Ridgedale Community in 1925.

these storms. Some people would actually leave when they saw an approaching storm. Church services were usually well attended, consisting of Baptists and Methodists. According to a former member Owen Prunty "You couldn't hardly tell us apart. We tended the Methodist Church and they'd tend our services. Our..preachers would come in and help the Methodists in their revivals. We all just worked together." There were usually church meetings held on Sunday and Sunday night with prayer meeting on one weekday night. Sunrise service was held on Easter and a special service on Christmas. In later years regular church meetings were held monthly. According to Earl Moody who was pastor from 1943

Chapter 10 Kyrock Church and School

This is a photo of the Kyrock Church Sunday School not long after the building was erected.

to 1947 mostly young people attended the church services and not very many men came. It was likely difficult for older people to climb the stairs up the steep hill and many of the men probably found little time to attend. Most people walked to church since only a few people owned automobiles. Dress was casual, consisting mostly of overalls for men and homemade dresses for the ladies.

Kyrock Methodist Church revivals lasted about eight to ten days and were attended by not only Methodists but also by Baptists. Many times the Baptist preachers helped in the revivals. The small differences in their beliefs apparently posed no insurmountable hindrance to working together. Those "saved" during a revival

This is an early photo of Kyrock Church Sunday School.

were given a choice of baptism by either being immersed in the nearby Nolin or Green River or being sprinkled as is customary by Methodists. As soon as Reverend Ogles became pastor in 1924 he and his wife began to publish a newsletter from the church called *The Kyrock Messenger*. Included in the publication were articles by the pastor, personal tidbits from the surrounding communities, obituaries, stories for children and other inspirational articles. No doubt this served as

Chapter 10   Kyrock Church and School

a popular means for keeping in touch with others around the area as well as keeping everyone informed of community affairs.

The company paid a small yearly salary, usually a few hundred dollars, to the pastor and was supplemented by donations from the church members and the church conference. Electricity, maintenance and other expenses were taken care of by the company. Kyrock Methodist Church was placed in the Bowling Green, Kentucky district of the Methodist church and was later included in the nearby Rocky Hill church circuit. Reverend Ogles continued his regular monthly route for two years until another pastor replaced him. Pastors usually stayed on the route for only one to two years before moving on to the next church. Membership increased from the original 13 to as much as 150 in 1948 and then slowly declined until the church was disbanded. As the Kentucky Rock Asphalt Company business began to decline, it could no longer provide money or expenses for the church. Without this support it became impossible for the church to operate. A resolution was passed in 1957 by the Louisville Annual Conference (of the Methodist Church) to "abandon the Church at Kyrock as a place of worship and instruct the Trustees of the annual Conference to sell the Church and turn over the proceeds to the District Board of Missions and Church Extension to be used in the Bowling Green District."

A group of the local Baptists purchased the building and its contents for $150. These materials were used to help build Kyrock Baptist Church located a short distance away on private property. The large bronze bell was also acquired, but was later stolen and no one knows what happened to it. Kyrock Baptist Church is still in operation and holds regular church services.

There were many fond memories of Kyrock Methodist Church. The fellowship and love of those who attended has been well documented and this helped bond the

Chapter 10   Kyrock Church and School

This is a photo of the dilapidated remains of the Kyrock Church after it was abandoned in 1957. Parts of the building and its contents were used to build Kyrock Baptist Church nearby.

community together during many difficult times. It was not unusual to hear prayers echo around the hills and hollows throughout the area during those years the church stood on top of that rocky hillside near the little village of Ridgedale.

Chapter 10   Kyrock Church and School

It was obvious from those who knew Mr. Carmichael that he was also a big proponent of education. He knew how difficult it was for many of the children living in the Kyrock communities to make what at times could be a long and difficult trip to attend school. There were no school buses to transport children to schools like Sweeden, Bee Spring or other nearby schools and most parents did not own automobiles. He made it a mission to establish a school nearby the Kyrock plant. Even with the Kyrock School it was not unusual for students to walk several miles to get to the school. By 1924 a small school building had been erected on company property down by the canal on a rare, relatively level piece of land. Most

This is a photo of the original Kyrock School built in 1924.

Chapter 10 **Kyrock Church and School**

important the school was fairly close to most of the residents in the area, especially most of those who had family members working at the Kyrock plant. In 1926 a two and a half story addition was built on to the original building to house high school students. Then in 1928 a separate building was erected nearby the original school to house high school students only.

This photo of the Jess Poteet family showing off their three sets of twins in front of the high school building appears to have been taken not long after the Kyrock High School was built.

Chapter 10 **Kyrock Church and School**

This is a photo (year unknown) of the students at Kyrock School.

According to former student Naomi Wilkins Williams the first Kyrock High School consisted of only three small rooms and one of those was used for the library and study hall. The elementary school had four rooms including the lunch room. The buildings were separated by the basketball court. There was no indoor plumbing and only outside toilets. Rooms were heated with coal stoves. The school buildings were painted the same forest green color as the other Kyrock buildings. Some of the students were allowed to skip eighth grade to increase the high school population and eventually the high school students and elementary students had to switch buildings to accommodate the increased high school population.

Chapter 10 Kyrock Church and School

This photo shows Kyrock High School as it appeared in the 1920's.

The Kyrock School was initially owned and operated by the Kyrock Plant which also paid teacher's salaries. A free primary school was established at the first school building and a kindergarten was set up in the Blue Town Hotel building in which parents could pay tuition for kindergarten children to attend. No records are available until operations at the school were taken over by the county in 1927 but there were probably no more than about 50 primary grade and 10 kindergarten students in the first year. No one could be found to teach at the school for the first

Chapter 10 **Kyrock Church and School**

year so Mr. Carmichael asked one of his Kyrock commissary employees Ezra Rich, who had 27 or 28 years of teaching experience and father of Lon Rich who later graduated from Kyrock, to take on the job. He was offered his full commissary salary as well as a teacher's salary. He accepted the job and persuaded his niece Lella Stewart to help him.

The first year as a public school was September 5, 1927 to March 31, 1928 and listed 61 boys and 52 girls ages six through fifteen crowded into one classroom with 48 seats. All students were placed in level 1 which was considered the primary block of instruction. In addition there were five boys and six girls attending kindergarten at the Blue Town Hotel during that year.

Early records for primary classes showed an emphasis on reading, writing and spelling but high school classes included a typical curriculum including courses in

This is a photo of the Kyrock High School class with Principal Harold McCombs ca. 1930. Notice the basketball goal and the court consisting of asphalt or dirt. The old Kyrock School was located just down the hill from this building.

Chapter 10   Kyrock Church and School

Algebra, Geometry, History, English and Geography. Classes began at precisely 8 AM ending at 4 PM with recesses at 10:00 AM and 2:30 PM and lunch at 12:00-1:00 PM. There was usually time for some extracurricular activities including special programs like school plays and the occasional good natured prank on teachers. There was usually a yearly trip for high school students to places like the Cincinnati Zoo or Grand Ol' Opry. Some heartwarming stories and accounts of those days at Kyrock School can be found in the book named *Kyrock Kentucky* published by Becky Lane Goad and the Library Ladies in 2010.

This shows the Senior Play announcement at Kyrock High School from March 26, 1943

Chapter 10   Kyrock Church and School

Special programs included singing, reciting poetry, pageants, chapel sessions, inspirational talks and dressing up in costumes or crepe paper dresses for some of these events. Sports activities like basketball, baseball and softball were all part of the Kyrock after school programs resulting in intense rivalries with local teams like Sunfish and Brownsville. Kyrock usually fielded competitive teams even while playing against schools with larger student populations. The first graduating class from Kyrock High School was in 1930 consisting of six students: Mabel Doyle, Clorene Harrison, Leslie Harrison, Alton Mitchell, Cecil Mitchell, and Arnold

This is a photo of one of the more competitive baseball teams from Kyrock High School that won the county tournament in 1939. Pictured back row, left to right: Ed Salley, Howard Doyle, Ed Lane, Snake Hogan, D.C. Sanders and Warren Lindsey; front row, left to right: Laymon Carroll, Red Meredith, Bill Houchin, Loyd (Pinkin) Jaggers, Leotis Harrod, Presque Lashley and Coach John Lane. They are posed in front of the old Kyrock School.

Chapter 10   Kyrock Church and School

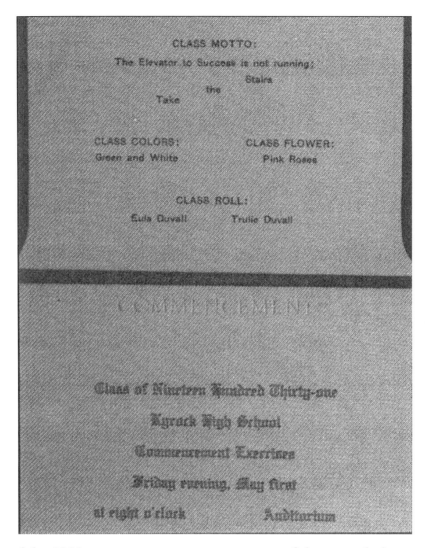

CLASS MOTTO:
The Elevator to Success is not running;
Take
the
Stairs

CLASS COLORS: CLASS FLOWER:
Green and White   Pink Roses

CLASS ROLL:
Eula Duvall   Trulie Duvall

COMMENCEMENT

Class of Nineteen Hundred Thirty-one

Kyrock High School

Commencement Exercises

Friday evening, May first

at eight o'clock   Auditorium

This is a copy of the 1931 commencement announcement of the second class to graduate from Kyrock High School. Only two students, Eula Duvall and Trulie Duvall, graduated in that class.

VanMeter.   The following year only two students, Eula Duvall and Trulie Duvall, graduated. In total there were 106 graduates listed in the final Kyrock Annual of 1947. Many former students went on to successful jobs and professions after attending the little Kyrock School. Others dropped out of school for various reasons prior to graduation from high school but everyone remembered their experience there with warm thoughts and pleasant memories.

In 1947-48 a new high school was built off Hwy 259 near Sweeden for the high school students. A gym was added in 1949-50 when some local residents and businessmen got together and raised the funds for the addition. That's the kind of spirit and support you might expect from the Kyrock community. The school currently houses the elementary grade students in kindergarten through eighth grade.

Chapter 11   Social Life and Entertainment

Work at the Kyrock plant and quarries was hard with long hours and difficult, sometimes backbreaking jobs, but it would be a mistake to think that there was no social life or entertainment for those who lived in and around Kyrock. Isolation from large towns or cities where there were things like movie theatres, sporting events or live performances by famous people did not mean that residents of the area never got to have those things. Mr. Carmichael understood that it was important that the Kyrock workers as well as people living around the area have social activities that would help them cope with the hard work. He did this not only out of concern for the success of the company, but also because he truly cared about the people in the area. It is obvious from comments made by former workers that he tried to provide as many company sponsored activities as possible.

Probably among the most remembered and celebrated events each year was at Christmas. A big old pine tree in front of the Kyrock Church was decorated and covered with lights. Santa Clause was played for many years by a colorful Kyrock worker named Albert Porter. He enjoyed playing the role enormously and would visit some of the nearby homes to ask the kids what they wanted for Christmas. A Christmas program was held near the old pine tree where every child who came was given a gift and a bag containing treats like an apple, orange, banana, candied peach slices, jelly beans and nuts. Adults received a gift, usually a sack of flour. Groups would sometimes gather to sing Christmas carols. You did not have to be a Kyrock worker to be part of the celebration. My mother recalled how thrilled she was to receive a doll one year at the Christmas celebration. In later years when Mr. Carmichael became ill he made the comment that at Christmas "I want these kids around here to have an apple and an orange and a bar of candy. I want that carried on and on and on and on when I'm gone." It meant a great deal to him

Chapter 11   Social Life and Entertainment

personally. Another holiday that the company helped sponsor was Easter. Money was provided by the company for the eggs and women in the community would prepare them. The field at the bottom of the hill from the church was used to hide the eggs. There would then be a big Easter egg hunt for the children.

Around the 4th of July each year the company would sponsor a picnic near the canal at Kyrock Landing. Hot dogs, cokes and cotton candy were provided to those attending. There would be games like a three-legged race or catching a greased pig. Rides up the river all the way to Mammoth Cave were provided either on the company's 35 foot cabin cruiser, a steam boat or a barge pulled by a small motor boat. One can only imagine the thrill of getting to take a scenic trip up the Nolin and Green Rivers, especially for the children.

Barge or Steamboat rides up the Nolin River were usually reserved for visitors but on special occasions such as the 4th of July local residents were allowed to take these rides.

Chapter 11 **Social Life and Entertainment**

These four photos show a celebration for the visit of Vice president Alben Barkley in 1949. Mr. Carmichael can be seen in the fourth photograph standing just behind the vice president.

.

Chapter 11 Social Life and Entertainment

When Kentucky Rock Asphalt Company was flourishing, its operations were visited by a group of state and county officials. In this 1938 photograph aboard steamer Nolin on Pigeon Creek are seated left to right Gov. A.B. "Happy Chandler", A.B. Mitchell, Chalybeate, representative of Edmonson and Butler Counties and Robert Humphrey, Mayfield, member of the Kentucky Highway Commission. Standing left to right are J. Boadley Davenport, Sheriff of Warren County; T.C. Ferguson, Smiths Grove, state senator; Kyrock Plant Superintendent H.T. St. G. Carmichael; Mr. Burnett; Emory G. Dent, Bowling Green, Kentucky Highway Commissioner; William H. Natcher, Warren County attorney; Cecil Whitehead, Bowling Green, Kentucky; Cecil Williams, Somerset member of Kentucky Highway Commission; Clyde Lester, representative, Graves County; Sinclair Davis; Two gentlemen unknown. On the lower deck is Mose Basham fireman on tow boat.

Chapter 11 **Social Life and Entertainment**

In the early days of Kyrock before good roads were accessible to the community most visitors used steamboats to make the trip. These photos show the steamboat Helen II bringing a load of well-dressed visitors to the plant. Most Kyrock inhabitants could not afford to ride these boats and had to use the dirt roads if there was a car available to make the trip.

156

Chapter 11 Social Life and Entertainment

In this photo an outside movie theatre can be seen with benches placed in front of a projection screen. It was located next to the commissary and later enclosed with an eight foot fence and roof. Eventually movies were shown at the grade school.

Since there were no movie theaters close to Kyrock, some of the workers decided to build their own. Former commissary worker Walter Davis recalled that he and a group of other Kyrock workers pooled their money by contributing about $200 each, which at that time was a considerable investment, to construct an open air movie theater near the commissary. They set posts in the ground and fastened 2x8 planks on them to form seats. They built a screen down the hill from the seats and located a projector at the upper end of the seating enclosed in a "little old shack". Eventually an 8-foot fence was built around the area and a roof was added. To recoup their investment the men charged ten cents for a ticket to watch the movie,

Chapter 11 Social Life and Entertainment

which were typically westerns, since they were by far the most popular. In later years movies were shown at the Kyrock Grade School building on Saturday nights. Many of the young as well as older folks liked to come see the movies even when they had to travel five or six miles and return home after dark.

Chautauqua shows were sometimes presented at Kyrock consisting of live performances by actors or perhaps magicians. Show boats would occasionally travel down the river to Kyrock to present live performances by some famous country music singers from the Grand Ol' Opry. Jean Wells Meredith recalled that for about ten cents people could board an old steam boat and watch performances by distinguished stars like Eddie Arnold, Roy Acuff and Pewee King. Occasionally Kyrock School would bring in magicians or trained dogs to perform for the children. Events like pie suppers to make up money for school activities were held and contests for the prettiest girl or the person with the dirtiest feet made for great entertainment.

Sports activities made up a large part of the entertainment for the community. The company built two regulation size tennis courts down near Kyrock Landing and paved them with asphalt from the plant. Anyone with a tennis racket and a ball could play there, although it was probably not as popular as some other sports such as baseball, softball and basketball.

There was an outside basketball court paved with asphalt next to the Kyrock High School. Both boys and girls Kyrock basketball teams practiced here and were known for their excellent passing skills. Their passing and shooting skills were most likely sharpened from lack of a gym since missed shots or errant passes usually meant chasing the ball down the steep hill down into the woods.

Chapter 11 Social Life and Entertainment

This is a photo of the tennis court built from Kyrock asphalt and located in one of the rare level fields near the canal. It provided a popular form of entertainment for residents who could locate a tennis racket and a ball.

Basketball games with seven local teams had to be held at the Brownsville gym usually played a couple of times each week during the season and ending with a well-attended tournament. Since Kyrock, Sunfish and Brownsville were the biggest schools it was usually very competitive games with those three schools.

Chapter 11 Social Life and Entertainment

Everyone really wanted to beat the Brownsville team since it was the county seat and had the most students.

Probably the most popular sport at Kyrock was baseball. School games were well attended with students walking up the steep hill from Kyrock School to the baseball field to watch the game before returning home. Since the school was small it was important to have as many students participate in sports as possible in order to form the teams. The Kyrock teams usually more than held their own against opposing teams. There were seven area teams that usually resulted in about two or three games per week during the season ending with a tournament at the end of the season. Games were popular with good crowds and fierce competition among all the teams.

It was also common to have baseball games start up at any time around the neighborhood when enough young people could be found to field a team, playing until darkness forced them to stop playing. Johnny Carmichael described how his dad, Mr. Carmichael, would many times summon him back home from a neighborhood game with a long-short-long honk of his car horn after which he would race home "as fast as a blue tail lizard".

It was common for mining companies in Appalachia and many southern states to sponsor baseball teams in their communities during the 1920's to around 1950. Games were extremely popular with workers as well as other folks in the community. Many of the players on these teams gained notoriety becoming stars around the mining communities. Some players occasionally found an opportunity to move up to professional teams. Mining companies found it beneficial to recruit and hire good baseball players. They were usually given easy jobs and paid for their time

Standing: Bill Garvin Sr., H.T. Carmichael, Garland James, Clyde Harrod, Stan Carmichael, Loren Lindsey, Bill Houchins, J.B. Patton (#9 unknown), and Lincoln Meredith. Seated: Glen Napper, John Carmichael, Ernest Thompson, Harold King, Hugh Bunnell, Paul Harrod, Hardin Doyle Jr., Willard Napper, and Bill Garvin Jr. This photo was taken in Louisville, Kentucky, circa summer of 1941 when Kyrock was runner-up to Eping (a team comprised of Greater Louisville All-Stars) in the State American Legion Championship

The top photo here is a team sponsored by Kyrock in 1941. Notice that Stan Carmichael is also on the team. The bottom photo shows the 1945 Boys Basketball team at the Old Kyrock School.

Chapter 11   Social Life and Entertainment

for practicing and playing. Kyrock also found it to be a positive thing for the community to sponsor a baseball team. Being a former baseball player himself Mr. Carmichael loved and promoted the sport. Even a building in the Kyrock production process was named the "bullpen". He would seek out the best baseball players from around the area to offer them jobs at Kyrock and the opportunity to play on the company baseball team. The technique worked because Kyrock usually had a great team that drew fans from the plant and nearby areas. Players like pitcher Nick Weaver who was six feet seven inches tall weighing 230 pounds was known for his no-hit games. Others like Wells Hackney and Buck Evans also became well known for their pitching ability.

To think that there was nothing around Kyrock for people to do would be a mistake. Not even considering the school and church activities there always seemed to be enough enjoyable activities around to occupy everyone's free time. The area was blessed with an outdoor person's paradise. There was plenty of fishing available on the Nolin and Green Rivers. There was an abundance of wild animals like deer, rabbits, squirrels and quail for hunting. The hills, hollows, bluffs and densely covered forests formed one of the most beautiful areas of the state. No doubt taken for granted by many, it was beloved by most who likely sacrificed a much better standard of living in some nearby city or town just to remain in the area. With a decent job, an opportunity to be near their home and an active social life most people considered Kyrock to be the best place in the world to spend their life.

Chapter 12 **Changing Times, Relocation and Closing**

During the great depression times were difficult in all areas of the country but people living in Kyrock had always been accustomed to hard times. Having a company like Kentucky Rock Asphalt present made times more bearable because there was a place there for people to work even if it meant reduced work due to the economy. Workers could charge necessities at the commissary during winter when work was stopped at the plant and work off their debt when the company reopened. This was unpopular with some of the workers because it gave those with debt at the commissary preference for work once it was restarted, but this practice was continued until the union was organized in 1937. Roads still had to be built and paved during the depression meaning there was still demand for Kyrock material. Mr. Carmichael kept the company as busy as he could by soliciting work from all over the country. With money in short supply the company implemented a system of scrip as payment during this time that could be used to purchase groceries and supplies at the commissary. Workers were grateful for even this since many others were waiting in unemployment lines or soup lines.

As effects of the depression began to ease, business for the company improved. Eventually the workers at Kyrock began to believe that wages at the plant were too low and working conditions needed to be improved. Some of the work could be very difficult and dangerous for the low wages. Many of the men had seen accidents where people had been killed there. Some of the men who lived around Kyrock began traveling to towns like Brandenburg, Kentucky near Louisville, Kentucky to find jobs such as pipe fitters making very good wages. The wages at Kyrock were probably much lower than those in larger cities or towns with similar jobs. When the plant began operations in 1919 the wage for general labor was

Chapter 12 Changing Times, Relocation and Closing

```
                                        Kyrock, Ky.,
                                        May 3rd,1922

Mr. Dover Williams,
Ohio Valley Rock Asphalt Co.,
Summit, Ky.

Dear Mr. Williams:-

                    Replying to your letter of May 1st
we are paying the following rates here:-

        Dinkey Skinners             36¢ Per Hour
        Brakemen                    20¢  "    "
        Experienced Brakemen capable
        of running dinkey in emergencies 25¢ "    "
        Powder Foremen              60¢  "    "
        Skilled helpers of long
        experience here             30¢  "    "
        Green Helpers               20¢  "    "
        Pipe Fitters in charge of lines
        Quarry No.1                 36¢  "    "
        Same in Morris Quarry
        Quarry(Light Work)          30¢  "    "
        All Shovel Pitmen           20¢  "    "
        Carpenters rated according to
        skill and experience        30¢ to 50¢ Per Hour

                    Am glad to note that you have
decided on a uniform scale of wages as am sure it will
work out advantageously.

                    We are in good shape to make
18000 buckets this month and will make it under
favorable weather conditions.

                    With warm regards and every good
wish, I am,
                    Sincerely Yours,

                    _____
```

This is a copy of a letter from Mr. Carmichael to another Rock Asphalt Company explaining the wage scale at the Kyrock Plant. Note that the base wage in 1922 was 20 cents per hour with more skilled or dangerous jobs paying a higher wage.

Chapter 12 Changing Times, Relocation and Closing

only about 14 cents per hour. For more skilled labor the rate went up 10 to 30 cents per hour higher. The base rate gradually rose to 17 1/2 cents per hour until in 1922 the lowest hourly rate was up to 20 cents per hour. This rate did not change very much over the next several years. Although not vocal, unrest among the workers began to take hold and a group of men from the plant began meeting in a barn near Sweeden to discuss the possibility of being represented by a Labor Union. In 1937 the workers decided to form a local union affiliated with the United Mine Workers. From most accounts Mr. Carmichael did nothing to fight against the unionization of the workers but it did make his job somewhat more difficult. He probably realized that the company wages and working conditions needed improvement but likely had little influence with company officials in higher positions to make any changes. After the plant became unionized the lower wage rate was raised from 20 to 25 cents per hour and other pay rates were adjusted higher. A seniority system was implemented for the workers that allowed those with seniority to have priority of work rather than give preference to those who were allowed to work off debt at the commissary. Not much was done to address working conditions or safety. Statistics from the U.S. Department of Commerce for 1937 listed average wages for quarry workers in 1936 in the south at about 37 cents per hour. Wages did not increase much in the United States from 1922 until 1936. The depression likely caused wages to be depressed during that time. Wages at Kyrock were probably still below national averages even after the wage increase in 1937. At any rate most workers at Kyrock preferred staying near their home to work even if it meant working for a little less money.

As the country moved into the decade of the 1940's however things began to

Chapter 12 Changing Times, Relocation and Closing

change for the company. World War II had begun which meant that many of the young men who would typically have worked at Kyrock were called to defend their country in the armed services. Some of those young men lost their lives in that endeavor causing much sadness in the community.

Over the years it became more difficult to find rock asphalt in the quarries near the plant with an ideal bitumen content of about 8 percent. The Black Gold quarry had been opened and that bitumen-rich rock asphalt was being transported about eight miles by dinkey over newly laid tracks from there to the processing plant. But as more and more of this rock was needed for transport the cost for doing this forced the company to consider relocating the processing plant closer to that quarry. In

Quarry operations were improved by using diesel powered shovels to load the rock into trucks for transporting to the crusher.

Chapter 12 Changing Times, Relocation and Closing

These two photos show the transfer and rebuilding of the Kyrock Processing Plant to its new location at Sweeden, Kentucky just across the road off Highway 259 (formerly Route 65) in 1946.

Chapter 12 Changing Times, Relocation and Closing

These two photos show how the Kyrock Plant appeared after the move to Sweeden, Kentucky. The crusher is located at the upper left hand side of the photos. The lower photo shows the finished product as it was moving down the chute on the right side.

168

Chapter 12 Changing Times, Relocation and Closing

In the 1940's and 1950's large diesel powered shovels were used to load the boulders of asphalt rock into trucks for transport from the quarry to the crusher located at Sweeden, Kentucky.

The large boulders of asphalt rock were dumped into the crusher at Sweeden, Kentucky. Contract haulers were used to haul the rock.

Chapter 12 Changing Times, Relocation and Closing

This is a photo of the large pile of finished rock asphalt located at the lower end of the Kyrock Processing Plant that was relocated to Sweeden, Kentucky. The derrick loaded trucks with this product that was hauled to the Rocky Hill, Kentucky distribution facility.

addition, trucks were beginning to be used to transport the rock asphalt. In 1946 the processing plant was moved just up the road to Sweeden across Highway 259. That year the final load of rock asphalt was hauled by barge to the distribution facility in Bowling Green, Kentucky. Thereafter the main distribution point became the Rocky Hill distribution facility. The use of dinkeys was gradually phased out in favor of trucks to haul the asphalt rock. Mining operations at the quarry became more automated with large shovels driven by diesel engines used to load the asphalt rock into trucks. These trucks were owned and operated by

Chapter 12 Changing Times, Relocation and Closing

contract workers who hauled the loads of asphalt rock to the crusher now located at Sweeden. The loads of large asphalt rocks were dumped into the crusher and processed by the same crushing and milling operations used at the old facility. The finished product which was subjected to the same rigorous testing procedures was moved by conveyor belt to a large pile of material at the bottom of the processing facility. A large derrick located near this pile of finished rock asphalt loaded the material into trucks. No longer were steamboats and barges needed to transport the product up the river to Bowling Green. It was transported by truck across the ferry at Brownsville, Kentucky to the Rocky Hill Distribution facility. In 1950 the bridge over Green River at Brownsville was completed making these shipments faster, easier and more economical. Workers were no longer needed to maintain and operate dinkeys or work on the rail line. Fewer workers were needed to load the material into trucks. By the late 1940's employment at Kyrock had dropped to about 200 workers. Business was still good but more competition was now being experienced with synthetic asphalt becoming popular and very competitive for paving roads. In 1949 Mr. Carmichael's health began to fail and on September 28 he passed away from uremic poisoning (kidney failure) and heart disease. His death was headlined in the Bowling Green Dailey News as "Man Who Led Effort to Save Collins Dies", but to those around Kyrock it meant much more than that. His contributions to Kyrock and the surrounding area were enormous. For almost thirty years he had been the man in charge serving as Plant Superintendent and later as Vice-president of Operations at the Kentucky Rock Asphalt Plant bringing it from near obscurity to a very successful operation. He was responsible for making the Kyrock community a more prosperous place by bringing some of the

Chapter 12 Changing Times, Relocation and Closing

This picture of Mr. Carmichael was taken not long before his death in 1949 at the age of 69.

Chapter 12 Changing Times, Relocation and Closing

more basic necessities to people in need of help. The Kentucky Chapter of the National Foundation for Infantile Paralysis in Louisville, Kentucky called his death "a tremendous loss" to their organization and said that his "excellent and extremely unselfish work for the crippled child is recognized throughout Kentucky". He had served as vice-chairman of the Kentucky chapter of the National Foundation for Infantile Paralysis since its organization in November, 1940 and as Kentucky chairman of the "March of Dimes" campaign for polio victims. He had also served as State Disaster Chairman for the Red Cross and Chairman of the Kentucky Planning Commission as well as being a member of the Public Works Commission. He was also a member of the board of trustees at his alma mater Washington and Lee University in Lexington, Virginia.

About three months before Mr. Carmichael's death he had been forced to leave his position at Kyrock due to his deteriorating health. Walter Salley became General Superintendent shortly thereafter and was later succeeded by Walter Bunnell. With all the knowledge and skill that later superintendents possessed they could not match the experience, knowledge and skill of Mr. Carmichael when it came to running the Kyrock Plant. It was becoming more difficult to economically manufacture the rock asphalt to compete with the synthetic hot melt blacktop. Mining and crushing the asphalt rock was difficult and labor intensive. Increased wages had made the labor cost more expensive and even with increased automation these costs made the material more costly. The quality of the Kyrock product began to become questionable with less care being taken in keeping out excess dirt from the finished product resulting in some of the blacktop roads using this material to quickly deteriorate. Business for Kyrock began to steadily decline dropping

Chapter 12 **Changing Times, Relocation and Closing**

This picture appeared in an article in the Louisville Courier Journal on June 22, 1957 announcing the Kyrock closing and showing the Kyrock processing facility at Sweeden. The remainder of this article shown below gave a rather gloomy description of the closing. The caption read as follows:

"This is Kentucky Rock Asphalt Company's crushing plant at Sweeden, which is off the picture to the left. The plant was moved here from the company town of Kyrock, about 2 miles, away back in 1946. Employment had dropped from about 600 to 200 during the peak mining season when it was decided to liquidate the firm."

Chapter 12 Changing Times, Relocation and Closing

EXIT KYROCK

Decision to dissolve the company hints hard times for employees and for all of Edmonson County

By JOE CREASON, Courier-Journal Staff Writer

SWEEDEN, Ky., June 22—No doubt about it, June 14 will be remembered as Black Friday in this little, oddly spelled ridge-country village in North-Central Edmonson County.

On that day, the stockholders of Kentucky Rock Asphalt Company voted to dissolve the corporation and go out of business after 40 years of supplying natural asphalt for road-building throughout the nation.

That action by the owners of the company is one that will be felt in the pocketbook, not just here, where the firm operated its crushing plant, but throughout Edmonson County, in at least two ways:

1. The closing of the operation, the county's only industry, means the loss of seasonal employment to 200 or more men.
2. It also means that the County, which has been in a tight financial predicament ever since nearly a fourth of its area was taken for Mammoth Cave National Park, has lost its second-largest tax source.

The decision to liquidate Kentucky Rock Asphalt and distribute its assets among the stockholders was easy to understand.

Wasn't Making Money

Although the supply of rock in the 4,500 acres the company holds in Edmonson County still is plentiful, and the country's greatest boom in road-building seems to be nearing, the firm simply wasn't making money. Moreover, the prospect of doing so in the future appeared slim.

In a letter to the 1,000 or more stockholders some weeks ago, H. H. Knight, company secretary, summarized:

"Your board of directors has become convinced that the business can no longer be operated successfully, and the board does not know of . . . any substantial chance of hereafter operating a business on a profitable basis."

the Nolin into the Green River, 33 miles down the Green to the mouth of the Barren, and 30 miles up that stream to Bowling Green.

Rock Applied Cold

Road builders were eager to get the natural rock asphalt because it differed from then still-new artifical asphalt, which is a compound of heavy oil residues, commonly mixed with crushed stone. The Kentucky rock, with its high content of natural asphalt, could be applied cold simply by being spread evenly on the road foundation and compressed to half its natural depth by steam rollers.

The village of Kyrock became a thriving community of a hundred or more houses, stores, and even a company hospital, the only hospital in the county.

New open-pit quarries were opened in other parts of the county. One underground operation was tried, but didn't pan out too well.

The last shipment was made by water in 1946. That same year, the crusher plant was moved from Kyrock to Sweeden (two "e's" are correct), an old settlement on Kentucky Route 65 that was founded by Swedish people. The next year, the company moved its headquarters from Louisville to Brownsville, the county seat. Kyrock became almost a ghost town.

In the years that followed, bad times set in. The introduction of cheaper road mixes cut deeply into sales. Profit dropped.

Finally, things reached such a state that the main sale of the rock was for use as an added material to make highways less slippery. This was achieved by applying the pulverized natural asphaltic limestone over a coating of hot asphalt.

Market Limited

The rock proved highly successful as a de-slicker, but the market was too limited within a 300- or 400-mile radius to keep the company going on the strength of such sales.

The liquidation agreed on last week was, in the opinion of the directors, the only possible

175

Chapter 12 Changing Times, Relocation and Closing

about 1/3 since 1949 and on June 14, 1957 the stockholders of the company decided that it was no longer profitable to keep Kyrock open voting to liquidate its assets. On August 8, 1958 it was announced that all common stock valued at only $311,823.90 would be distributed to stockholders. Explanations for the closing included competition from synthetic asphalt, high labor cost, inability to hold up to the increased loads from boxcar sized trucks and illness of G. H. Bechill, the man in charge of the operation. Many around Kyrock believed the closing was directly related to the death of Mr. Carmichael.

Chapter 13   The Remains of An Era

After the closing of the Kyrock facility all its assets were liquidated by 1957. The company owned houses and lots along with most of the company owned land were sold. Reynolds Associates acquired the mineral rights and several thousand acres of land formerly owned by Kyrock.

Attempts were made on different occasions to mine and utilize product from the former facility, but with limited success. In the 1960's attempts were made to use the lean processed Kyrock material (4% bitumen) as a base for construction of rural roads, but with little success. In 1965 an experiment was run on the newly constructed Nolin Dam road using the lean Kyrock material as a base and a hot mix enriched Kyrock surface. Unfortunately the experiment failed due to the instability of the low bitumen base resulting in cracks and breakage. In 1966 a company named Gripstop Corporation was formed and worked with the Kentucky Department of Highways (KDOH) to manufacture a re-surfacing product using Kyrock material with the excellent non-skid properties. The lean Kyrock material containing only about 4% bitumen was enriched with 5% paving grade asphalt to form a mix applied by conventional hot mix paving methods. After about five to six years roads paved with this material were evaluated and results were shown to be very good especially in respect to its anti-skid properties. However, there were air pollution problems in processing the material when it was heated and other handling problems that could not be adequately resolved. Production ceased in 1970 with no further attempts to revive the production until 1992 when the Kentucky Transportation Center in cooperation with the Kentucky Transportation Department and Center for Applied Energy Research at the University of Kentucky conducted a study to again evaluate the use of Kyrock material as an ingredient in a paving mixture for Kentucky roads that would not only improve skid resistance but also reduce the cost of the paving material. A plan to utilize the techniques discovered in the study was abandoned when the owner of the Kyrock properties and the paving contractor were unable to agree on some of the provisions of the project. In 2003 interest again arose when the Kentucky Transportation Center at the University of Kentucky contacted the Kentucky Transportation Cabinet and again asked for the Kyrock material to again be considered as an additive to asphalt being used in paving some Kentucky roads. Advantages were listed as its durability, high skid resistance, reduction of material costs and benefits to the local economy. In 2004 a company named Hart County Stone re-opened the Indian Creek Quarry and began mining the material for tests to again evaluate the Kyrock

This sign just off Highway 259 near Sweeden, Kentucky marks the entrance to the Indian Creek Quarry formerly owned by Kyrock. In 2008 Kyrock material was being mined and processed at this site.

Chapter 13   **The Remains of An Era**

The top photo shows asphalt rock being extracted from the nearby cliff while in the bottom photo these boulders are being dumped into equipment for crushing and processing by Hart County Stone.

179

Chapter 13 **The Remains of An Era**

This photo shows the piles of crushed asphalt rock processed by Hart County Stone awaiting shipment to a facility where it will be used as part of an asphalt mix for road paving.

material as a possible additive for asphalt paving material. In 2009 Glass Construction began leasing the Indian Creek Quarry to mine it for mixing with asphalt for paving. No further actions have been found.

There is very little remaining of the original Kyrock facility or other former structures that were once part of the once thriving community. If you drive down Highway 259 N (formerly Route 65) toward Sweeden, Kentucky and take a right turn on the Old Kyrock Road you will only travel a few miles to a dead end. At this point just before the road ends the Kyrock Log Hotel was formerly located but now has been overgrown with trees and brush. If the old road was still open it

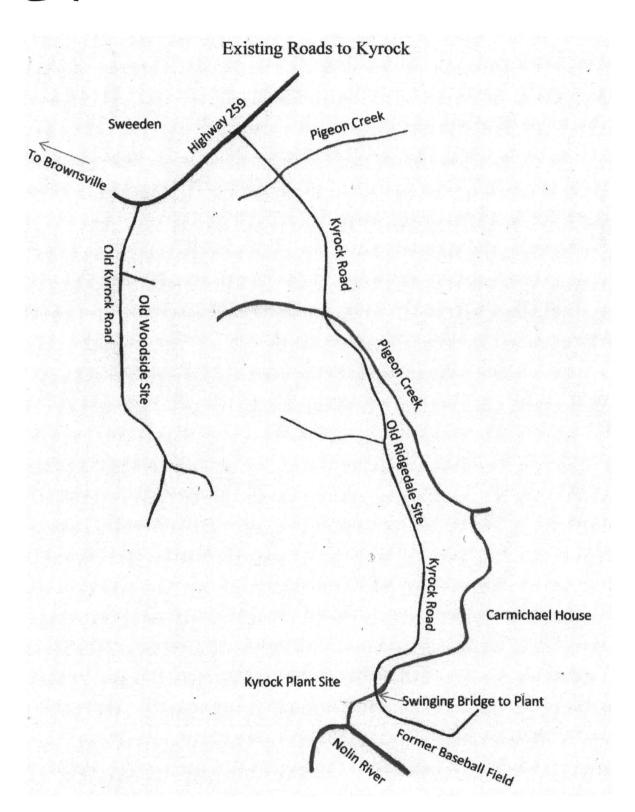

Existing Roads to Kyrock

Sweeden

Highway 259

To Brownsville

Pigeon Creek

Kyrock Road

Old Kyrock Road

Old Woodside Site

Pigeon Creek

Old Ridgedale Site

Kyrock Road

Carmichael House

Kyrock Plant Site

Swinging Bridge to Plant

Former Baseball Field

Nolin River

The top photo shows where the old Log Hotel once stood now overgrown and the bottom photo shows where the road once led to the Woodside Community but now is blocked.

Chapter 13   The Remains of An Era

The top photo shows the field where Ridgedale community once stood while the bottom photo shows the location of the once Kyrock Church on the hill above Ridgedale.

Chapter 13   The Remains of An Era

This photo shows where Kyrock Church was located. Note the concrete pillars are all that now remain of the church building. It is said that the church sat on 13 of these pillars representing the thirteen Disciples of Christ.

would lead to where the Woodside community was once located and eventually to the Ridgedale community. From there the road leads to the Kyrock Plant only accessible now by turning around and heading back to Highway 259 towards the New Kyrock Road. Turning right there then leads to an open field where the Ridgedale community was once located. Traveling further down this road takes you to Pigeon Creek and Sweet Spring. The Kyrock plant was located just to the right at this location just above the canal where barges were once loaded with Kyrock finished material. You can still see the concrete pylons nearby that supported the swinging bridge. An access road nearby on the left leads to Mr. Carmichael's

Chapter 13 The Remains of An Era

The Carmichael house is the only structure remaining from the Kryock era.

The concrete pylons once holding the swinging bridge can still be seen from Kyrock Road.

Chapter 13   The Remains of An Era

The water tower that furnished water for the Kyrock plant and some of the houses is still standing and can barely be seen from the road.

former house, the last remaining structure of Kyrock. It is currently being renovated by the owner Larry (Butch) Carol to match the original building as closely as possible. If you stay on Kyrock Road further it follows closely where the Bluetown community was located. River Road lay just below here nearby the Nolin River on the right side. The Commissary and Office building were located in this area, but no trace of them remains. Continuing on you will pass by a field on the right that was used for the baseball games so popular at the time Kyrock was in full operation. If you travel back to Highway 259 toward Sweeden and turn left toward Brownsville you will notice an area to the right just before getting to the Volunteer

Chapter 13   The Remains of An Era

This photo shows the road once leading down to the Kyrock plant relocated to Sweeden.

Fire Department. Down a slight grade from the Fire Department is where the Ky-rock Plant was relocated in 1946. It has become overgrown with very little remaining from the Sweeden plant. If you proceed down this pathway and slightly to the right you will find what remains of the last processing plant for Kyrock. Most of what remains is very overgrown but still contains the remains of some of the buildings. You can still see where the stockpiles of finished Kyrock material was stored and readied for shipment.

Although not much remains of the former plant and town of Kyrock where at one time about 2000 people lived, worked and attended school, there is still a lot of pride in those who remember that era. As memories fade and people who lived there pass away it becomes more difficult to keep those memories from being lost. A few artifacts and documents are on display at the existing Kyrock Elementary

Chapter 13   The Remains of An Era

This photo shows the remains of part of the processing plant that was relocated in 1946 to Sweeden just across Highway 259.

School just off Highway 259, but not much has been written to document those precious memories of Kyrock. The *Kyrock Kentucky* book with many heartwarming stories, photos and firsthand accounts was published in 2010 by Becky Lane and the Library Ladies. A group of friends and relatives of those who lived at Kyrock have a yearly Kyrock Day and come to share stories, photos and memories of those times, but it's unsure how long this tradition will continue since the number of those who still remember those days at Kyrock becomes smaller each year. It is my hope that this pictorial history of Kyrock can be a small part of keeping those memories alive.

Chapter 13   The Remains of An Era

Above are some of the artifacts on display at Kyrock Elementary School. Top left is an engraved stone once located at Kyrock, top right core samples once used by Kyrock, lower left a trophy of the 1931 basketball team and lower right a pin from one of the annual Kyrock Day celebrations.

Chapter 13   The Remains of An Era

This monument was erected outside the New Kyrock School building off Highway 259 to commemorate the contributions of Mr. Carmichael to the Kyrock Community. It reads: "In Memory of Harry St. George Tucker Carmichael Engineer Philosopher Humanitarian. Erected by a grateful people to honor his love, labor and leadership."

Bibliography

Allen, David L. "Use of Kentucky Rock Asphalt." Letter to Kentucky Transportation Cabinet, Lexington, KY: University of Kentucky, 2003.

Carmichael P.E., H. St. G. T. "The Asphalt Industry of Kentucky". Letter response to David W. Hayes. May 28, 1969.

Carmichael, Stanrod, interview by Ernie Elmore. Kyrock and Mr. Carmichael June 7, 2010.

Carmichael, Stanrod. S.T.C. (Memoirs) Atlanta, GA, June 3, 2004.

Company, Ajax Coal, interview by Harry St. G. T. Carmichael. Work Solicitation (August 17, 1922).

Creason, Joe. "Exit Kyrock". The Courier Journal. June 23, 1957.

Day-Lindsey Lisa. "Kyrock Quarry: The Solid Rock of Edmonson County". The Kentucky Explorer. March 2004 18-20.

Dick, J. A. "Panoramic Photo History and A Man Named John Dick-Day 26." JellyJumble.com (Photo provided by Library of Congess). Nov. 1918. http://jellyjumbles.com/?p=1954 (accessed Aug. 16, 2015).

Dunn, Frank C. (editor). "Kentucky Rock Asphalt Company." Kentucky Progress Oct. 1930: Vol III No. 2.

Goad, Becky. *Kyrock Kentucky*. Horse Cave, Kentucky Cave Country Print Shop, Div. of Jobe Publishing Inc. 2010.

Bibliography

Hagan, Wallace W. "Sedimentology of the Kyrock Sandstone (Pennsylvanian) In the Brownsville Paleo Valley Edmonson and Hart Counties, Kentucky". Kentucky Geological Survey. University of Kentucky Series X, 1978.

Hayes, David W. "Kentucky's Rock Asphalt Industry Gave Birth to Community of Kyrock". Kentucky Explorer. Sept. 1995 33-36.

Jillson, Willard Rouse. "Oil, Gas, Coal, Asphalt and Fluorspar Fields". Kentucky Geological Survey Series VI 1927 pp 3, 5.

Kentucky Rock Asphalt Co. "Kyrock". Circa 1924.

Kentucky Rock Asphalt Co. "The Kyrock Book". Kyrock Uniform Pavement. Circa 1928.

Kentucky Rock Asphalt Co. "The Story of Kyrock". Circa 1928 1-16.

Kentucky Rock Asphalt Company. "Kentucky Natural Sandstone Rock Asphalt." Specifications and Designs for its many uses in Construction and Maintenance, 1944: 1-5.

LeSieur, Jack. "A Road to the Past." The Assessment of the Archaelogical and Oral History of The Kentucky Rock Asphalt Company., Bowling Green, KY: Western Kentucky University, 2012.

Marks, Mary E. "The Rock Asphalt Industry of Western Kentucky". Dissertation to Graduate Faculty in Candidacy For The Degree of Master Of Science, The University of Chicago. Dec. 1931.

Bibliography

Merritt, Dixon. "Construction of the City of Old Hickory". "In SONS OF MARTHA," by Dixon Merritt, Chapter XVII. New York City: Mason & Hangar, 1928.

Minor, Robyn L. "Kyrock May Be on a Roll." Bowling Green Daily News, July 3, 2009.

Montell, Dr. Lynwood. *Kyrock Oral History Project*. Interviews written and summarized by students., Bowling Green, KY: Western Kentucky University Dept. of Folkland and Intercultural Studies, 1981.

Newell, Willian. "Interesting Historical Facts About Old Hickory and the Nashville Industrial Corp." The Old Hickory News, Mar. 29, 1929.

Noger, Martin C. "Tar Sand Resources of Western Kentucky". Kentucky Geological Survey Series XI 1999 1.

Ogles, H. C. "Death of Col. Malcolm H. Crump." The Kyrock Messenger, Feb. 1925: Vol. 2 No. 2.

Owen, David Dale. "General Report of Geological Survey". Kentucky Geological Survey. 1854/55 166.

Roper, Daniel C. "Statistical Abstract of the United States 1937." U.S. Department of Commerce. Washington D.C.: United States Government Printing Office, 1938.

Rose, Jerry G. "Kentucky Rock Asphalt (Kyrock) Road Surfacing Material." Research Report, Lexington, KY: University of Kentucky, 1992.

Bibliography

Sisco, Scott. "Hart County Stone applies to mine kyrock from old Edmonson County site." Bowling Green Daily News, March 30, 2004: 3A.

Unknown. "H.T. Carmichael '99 Humanitarian." The Alumni Magazine Washington and Lee University, 1925: 11.

Unknown (GenDisasters.com). "Jacksonville, TN Old Hickory Powder Plant Fire, Aug. 1924." The Washington Post, Aug 11, 1924.

Unknown. The Associated Press. "Man Who Led Effort To Save Collins Dies." Bowling Green Daily News, Sept. 29, 1949.

Wikipedia.org. Dec. 20, 2015. https://en.wikipedia.org/wiki/M._M._Logan (accessed Dec. 2015).

Williams, Dover, Wage Rates. Letter by Harry St. G. T. Carmichael. May 3, 1922.

Acknowledgements

Compiling photos and information about Kyrock was sometimes difficult. This task was made easier with the help of some kind and generous people.

Becky Goad who was responsible for publishing *Kyrock Kentucky* in 2010 was extremely helpful in providing many photos and other information on Kyrock. Her knowledge of Kyrock is extensive.

Kenneth Ashley was very helpful by providing copies of some of the Kyrock photos. His input on some of those photos was extremely helpful. We also retraced roads and former locations of structures located at the old Kyrock plant site and at Sweeden.

Joan Skaggs, whose father Clarence Harrison was the deliveryman for Kyrock, gave me many photos and other information about Kyrock.

Stanrod Carmichael, son of Harry Carmichael, provided some personal accounts of his father and the photo of him in his baseball uniform. His conversation and appearance somewhat reminded me of how his father might have once talked and looked. He passed away about a year after I interviewed him at the nursing home in Atlanta, GA.

Chris Carmichael, son of John Carmichael and grandson of Harry Carmichael, provided some invaluable information and photos of Mr. Carmichael. He currently lives in Bowling Green, KY.

Larry (Butch) Carrol, the current owner of the old Carmichael house gave me photos and other information on Kyrock. He also opened up the Carmichael house for the Kyrock reunion and allowed us to tour the house and grounds.

Marilyn Davis, whose father Percy Davis was a former employee of Kyrock, allowed me to listen to the recording of her father that was made by Mark Ames

Acknowledgements

when he interviewed Mr. Davis for the Kyrock Oral History Project on Feb. 26, 1981.

Western Kentucky University, Kentucky Library and Museum was a very good source for copies of photos, periodicals and other reference materials on Kyrock. One source in particular was the Kyrock Oral History Project conducted in 1981 by a group of students at Western. This project was an extensive research project supervised by Dr. Lynwood Montell in which the following students interviewed former employees and residents of the Kyrock area and collected a large amount of information:

Interviewer	Interviewee
Jan Alm	Lon Rich, William B. Lane, Sr. and Jean W. Meredith
Mark Ames	Percy Davis, Anderson Lashley, Herbert Harp, Gilbert Davis, Mrs. Gilbert Davis and Obed Crowder
Lorama Davis	Earl Moody, Owen Prunty and Naomi Meredith
Kevin Hunter	Charles Ray, Julius Cardwell, James F Madison and Lon Rich
Sheila Riley	Rosie L. Harrison, Clarence Harrison, Walter F. Davis, Romer Lindsey and John Carmichael
Alice Vinson	Julius Cardwell, Cordie Dunn, Walter Gipson and Roy Hazlip

Recordings and transcripts of these interviews are located in the Folklore and Folklife section in the Kentucky Library.

56815867R00112

Made in the USA
Lexington, KY
30 October 2016